SMALL BITES

PAUL GAYLER

SMALL BITES

TAPAS, MEZZE AND OTHER TASTY MORSELS

PHOTOGRAPHY BY PETER CASSIDY

KYLE BOOKS

To Anita, with love

This edition published in Great Britain in 2015 by Kyle Books, an imprint of Kyle Cathie Ltd.

192–198 Vauxhall Bridge Road, London SW1V 1DX general.enquiries@kylebooks.com www.kylebooks.com

First published in Great Britain in 2007 under the title *The World in Bite Size*

10 9 8 7 6 5 4 3 2 1   ISBN 978-0-85783-287-0

Text © 2007 Paul Gayler Photography © 2007 Peter Cassidy Book design © 2007 Kyle Books

Project editor Jennifer Wheatley   **Designer** Jane Humphrey   **Photographer** Peter Cassidy (see also page 192)   **Home economist** Linda Tubby   **Styling** Róisín Nield (apart from pages 20, 27, 41, 58, 103, 148–151, 183; Helen Trent)   **Copy editor** Emily Hatchwell   **Editorial assistant** Vicki Murrell   **Production** Sha Huxtable and Alice Holloway

Paul Gayler is hereby identified as the author of this work in accordance with Section 77 of the Copyright, Designs and Patents Act 1988.

A Cataloguing In Publication record for this title is available from the British Library.

Colour reproduction by Chromographics Printed and bound in China by C&C Offset Printing Co., Ltd.

Recipe photographs refer to the first recipe featured on the facing page

small eating is becoming a big deal. No longer do we have to sit down to a three-course meal whenever we eat out. Instead, more and more restaurants are offering a menu of 'small plates', from which we can mix and match as we please.

Little bites of food amuse, stimulate and excite the palate. They give both the cook and the diner an opportunity to experiment with a variety of different ingredients, and there is always something to suit everyone's taste – perfect for people who can never make up their mind!

The phenomenon of bite-size eating isn't new. It has its roots in some of the world's greatest cuisines: think of the tapas of Spain, the antipasti of Italy, the dim sum of China, the tiffin of India and the mezze of the Middle East. What is new, however, is that these little dishes are now becoming the main event, rather than just something to awaken the appetite before a meal. For diners, it's a relaxed and sociable way of eating. For chefs, it's an inspiring way to cook – an opportunity to play around with tastes, textures and flavours without being constrained by the conventions of the three-course meal.

Bite-size eating was born out of Spanish tapas, which are thought to have originated in Andalucía several hundred years ago. A piece of bread or cured meat, or some olives or nuts, was placed on a saucer on top of glasses to stop flies from getting in the drink (the word *tapar* means 'to cover'). This evolved to include more elaborate dishes, such as tortilla (potato omelette), *patatas bravas* (fried potatoes with a spicy tomato sauce) and grilled shellfish and sausages. It's customary in Spain to move from one bar to another sampling the different fare, which is always accompanied by a glass of wine or sherry. A similar ritual takes place in Venice, where bar snacks known as *cicchetti* are eaten with a glass of wine between meals. It's a sociable ritual, where meeting up with friends and chatting about the events of the day are the priority, and little plates of food help to assuage hunger and temper the effects of alcohol.

Perhaps the Mediterranean climate encourages this kind of eating. When the sun's beating down it's more tempting to nibble at an assortment of little dishes than to embark on a big meal. The countries of the Eastern Mediterranean have their own version of 'small-plate' eating, in the form of mezze. Laden with fragrantly spiced little dishes, the mezze table is an awesome sight: smooth, creamy purées such as hummus, taramasalata and baba ghanoush; elegant pastries such as *spanokopitta*, filled with meat, vegetables or cheese; rustic salads and smoky grilled vegetables; crisp fritters of seafood or fish, served with little sauces for dipping – all garnished with fresh herbs and enlivened with the warm, aromatic spices of the region. What was once intended to start a meal has become the main feature.

The Far East, too, has a long tradition of small bites. Street vendors throughout the region sell delicacies that can be held in the hand and are easy to eat. Then there's the great tradition of dim sum, originating in China's tea houses, where a feast of bite-size food is wheeled to your table on trolleys stacked high with bamboo baskets: buns stuffed with roast pork, translucent little dumplings filled with prawns, spring rolls, little croquettes, steamed spare ribs, and much more. Dim sum has become hugely popular in the West, matched only by the craze for sushi. Once street food in Japan, eaten by the poor, sushi is now big business, and is so successful in the West that it has been described as 'Japanese tapas'. Conveyor-belt sushi restaurants, where tempting little morsels are prepared in front of your eyes and then moved slowly past you in a mesmerising procession, are all the rage. Unlike the tapas bar with its convivial atmosphere, these restaurants can feel functional and canteen-like. But they feed the never-ending appetite for small plates, and for a new, informal, deconstructed way of eating.

how to serve bite-size food Small plates of food are a fantastic way to entertain at home, and perfectly suited to today's casual style of eating. A well thought-out selection of bite-size foods can easily replace a more traditional offering, whether you serve them for a sit-down meal or buffet style, with drinks. Sharing plates of food is a sociable, informal affair, and passing the plates around breaks down barriers and encourages conversation.

Here are a few points to bear in mind when planning a 'bite-size' meal:

– Keep the dishes small – they look more tempting this way, and they are also easier to serve, either by fork or spoon, or by hand.

– Aim to achieve a mix of colours, tastes and textures, so that all the dishes look as enticing as possible.

– Vary the cooking techniques, both to make things easier for yourself and to provide a pleasing selection for your guests – for example, a couple of dishes might be baked in the oven, a couple fried or grilled, and you could also serve some salads and breads.

– Stay true to one cuisine, so the meal has some coherence – don't mix Spanish tapas with dim sum, for example!

– Modern presentation can be a lot of fun, so be sure to use a range of unusual dishes, deep bowls, glasses, spoons or skewers.

– Remember, you don't even have to cook at all. A simple tapas selection could consist of some good olives and salted almonds, piquillo peppers, an assortment of cured meats, a couple of cheeses, and some bread and salad.

– As with all simple things, good-quality ingredients are key.

In this book I have tried to create an exciting and varied selection of recipes. I hope it inspires you to experience for yourself the wonderful flavours that small-plate eating has to offer. There are simple dishes, quickly cooked on the grill or in a wok, some light, some more robust. Other dishes are more complex, but very rewarding. I have been careful to respect culinary traditions but occasionally I like to fuse flavours and techniques.

serving sizes The recipes are designed to serve four people an appetiser-size portion; if necessary, you can double the quantities to serve as a main dish.

the americas

Mexico has its *botanas*, Colombia its *pasabocas* and Argentina its *picadas* – a long tradition of delicious bite-size snacks served in markets, bars and cafés, enticing passers-by with their pungent aromas and bright, fresh colours.

Fruit shop, Playa del Carmen, Mexico

louisiana crab hash

250g fresh white crabmeat (excess water squeezed out)
½ teaspoon green Tabasco sauce
2 spring onions *finely chopped*
1 teaspoon ground cumin
2 tablespoons freshly chopped coriander
75g tinned sweetcorn *drained*
150g mashed potato
1 egg *beaten*
100g panko (Japanese-style breadcrumbs)
sea salt and freshly ground black pepper
virgin olive oil, for frying
garlic mayonnaise, to serve

One of the highlights of travelling to America over the years has been visiting the Deep South, with its mélange of cuisines. I created this dish based on a Louisiana-style crabcake recipe. Simply dig in with a fork before everybody else gets to it.

1 Place the crabmeat, Tabasco, spring onions, cumin, coriander and sweetcorn in a bowl, mix well and season to taste. Add the mashed potato, then the egg and the crumbs. Adjust the seasoning again and mix well.

2 Heat a small, shallow-sided omelette pan with a little olive oil. When hot, add the crab mixture, pressing it down to fill the base of the pan. Fry until golden, about 2–3 minutes, then crush it lightly, fold over the outside to the centre, and fry again for a further 2–3 minutes, until the mixture is slightly crusty in appearance.

3 Turn out the hash into a bowl and allow to cool slightly before cutting it into wedges. Serve with the garlic mayonnaise.

pg tip Japanese-style breadcrumbs, or panko, are coarse in texture and beautifully light and crisp when fried. They are available in good supermarkets and Oriental grocery stores, but you can make your own version at home. Spread some coarse white breadcrumbs in a baking tray and bake in the oven, at 160°C/325°F/gas mark 3, stirring often, until they are crisp but not brown. This takes 8–10 minutes.

25ml buttermilk (or milk)

1 large egg white *lightly beaten until foamy*

¼ teaspoon garlic salt

⅛ teaspoon paprika

dash of Tabasco sauce

125g plain flour

½ teaspoon cayenne pepper

sea salt and freshly ground black pepper

300g cooked crayfish tails or small prawns *drained*

vegetable oil, for deep-frying

cajun popcorn

You should be able to buy cooked crayfish tails in brine from your fishmonger, but small Norwegian prawns would also fit the bill nicely. The crispy crayfish cry out to be dunked in a spicy dip: try jazzing up a good-quality mayonnaise with a little Cajun spice, or tomato ketchup with a few drops of Tabasco.

1 In a bowl, combine the milk, egg, garlic salt, paprika and Tabasco. Place the flour in another bowl and season with the cayenne, salt and pepper.

2 Dip the crayfish tails in the milk mixture, then dredge them in the seasoned flour.

3 Heat the vegetable oil to 180°C/350°F, immerse the crayfish into the hot oil and fry until golden and crispy. Remove with a slotted spoon and drain on kitchen paper.

50g fine cornmeal

50g plain flour

1 teaspoon caster sugar

1 teaspoon baking powder

sea salt and freshly ground black pepper

1 egg *beaten*

120ml milk

8 large hot dog sausages (e.g. Frankfurters, or merguez if you prefer)

vegetable oil, for deep-frying

mustard, to serve

corn dogs

A corn dog is basically a hot dog coated in a cornmeal batter and deep-fried (though it can also be baked). Most corn dogs are served on wooden skewers nowadays, but the original one – apparently invented in Minnesota in 1941 – presumably was not!

1 In a bowl, combine the cornmeal, flour, sugar and baking powder, and season with salt and pepper. Beat in the egg and milk to form a batter, then leave to stand for 30 minutes.

2 Spear each hot dog sausage lengthways with a soaked bamboo skewer, leaving enough protruding for a handle.

3 Heat the vegetable oil in a frying pan to 150°C/300°F. Dip each hot dog into the batter and then immerse into the hot oil. Fry until golden and crispy then remove with a slotted spoon. Drain on kitchen paper.

4 Serve with your favourite mustard.

300ml concentrated orange juice
1 tablespoon hot pepper sauce
200ml white wine vinegar
3 garlic cloves *crushed*
1 tablespoon dried oregano
½ tablespoon cumin seeds
1 tablespoon annatto seeds (optional)
2 tablespoons vegetable oil
750g pork belly *skinned and boned*
150ml dark beer
8 flour tortillas

for the pickle
50g caster sugar
100ml rice wine vinegar
2 red onions *very thinly sliced*

rolled pork burritos

Cooking pork in beer, peppers and orange may sound unlikely, but believe me it really works. Make sure that after cooking the pork you bind it well in the reduced cooking juices, as this helps to keep the meat juicy and moist.

1 Preheat the oven to 180°C/350°F/gas mark 4.

2 In a blender, blitz together the orange juice, pepper sauce, vinegar, garlic, oregano, cumin and annatto seeds (if using).

3 Heat the oil in a flameproof casserole, then add the pork and seal it all over. Pour over the beer, along with the contents of the blender. Cover with a lid and place in the oven to braise for 1–1½ hours, or until the meat is very tender.

4 Meanwhile, make the pickle. Boil the sugar and vinegar in a pan together for 2–3 minutes, then pour over the onions in a bowl. Leave to cool.

5 When the pork is cooked, lift it out into a large bowl and shred the meat with two forks. Meanwhile, place the sauce from the casserole into a pan and reduce until thick enough to coat the meat.

6 To serve, simply roll up the shredded pork in the tortillas, cut them in half, and top with the onion pickle.

8 small chicken drumsticks
1 small onion *finely chopped*
1 red chilli *deseeded and finely chopped*
2 tablespoons Monterey Jack cheese (or mature Cheddar) *grated*
75g merguez sausage (or fresh chorizo) *very finely diced*
3 tablespoons virgin olive oil
8 rashers streaky bacon
sea salt and freshly ground black pepper
2 tablespoons runny honey
2 tablespoons dark soy sauce
freshly chopped coriander, to serve

tex mex chicken

The spicy merguez sausage originates in North Africa, but it is used extensively in Latin cooking. I love it immensely. The smokiness of the sausage's chilli-pork base goes superbly with the chicken in this recipe.

1 Firstly, you need to bone the drumsticks. Starting with the knee joint, carefully separate the chicken meat from the bone with the tip of a small knife. Follow the bone up, keeping the flesh intact until you reach the top of the drumstick.
2 Roll back the flesh and, carefully, using a large chopping knife, cut off the bone about 1cm from the top. This should give you a boned-out drumstick with just a small piece of bone protruding at one end. (A friendly butcher will do this if necessary!)
3 Mix the onion, chilli, cheese, merguez and half the oil together in a bowl, then use this mixture to fill each drumstick cavity. Wrap each drumstick in a rasher of bacon and then secure with a cocktail stick. Season liberally.
4 Heat a grill pan until hot. Brush the drumsticks with the remaining oil, place on the grill and cook for 10–12 minutes.
5 Boil the honey and soy sauce together in a pan and brush this mixture liberally onto the chicken drumsticks as they cook. Serve sprinkled with the coriander.

pg tip These chicken drumsticks are delicious served with a spicy tomato ketchup, made by simply adding a little creamed horseradish and a squeeze of lemon juice to regular tomato ketchup.

½ teaspoon Tabasco sauce

1 teaspoon Worcestershire sauce

1 teaspoon soy sauce

2 tablespoons chopped flat-leaf parsley

1 small red chilli *finely chopped*

1 small onion *chopped*

1 teaspoon cayenne pepper

1 teaspoon garlic salt

500g chicken wings

4 tablespoons tomato ketchup

for the dip

100ml sour cream

50g blue cheese *grated*

buffalo hot wings

Chicken wings are eaten in many forms throughout the world, but for me the buffalo style takes a lot of beating – but then again I am a great spice lover.

1 Mix all the ingredients (except the chicken and the tomato ketchup) together in a bowl. Place the chicken wings in the marinade and leave for 1 hour.

2 Preheat the oven to 180°C/350°F/gas mark 4.

3 Transfer the contents of the bowl to a roasting tin and place in the oven for 30–35 minutes, turning the wings occasionally. When cooked, remove from the oven and leave to cool slightly.

4 Heat a grill pan until very hot, place the wings on the grill, and cook for a further 5 minutes. Mix the tomato ketchup with a little of the cooking marinade and use this to baste the wings as they cook.

5 Mix together the sour cream and blue cheese and serve alongside the hot wings.

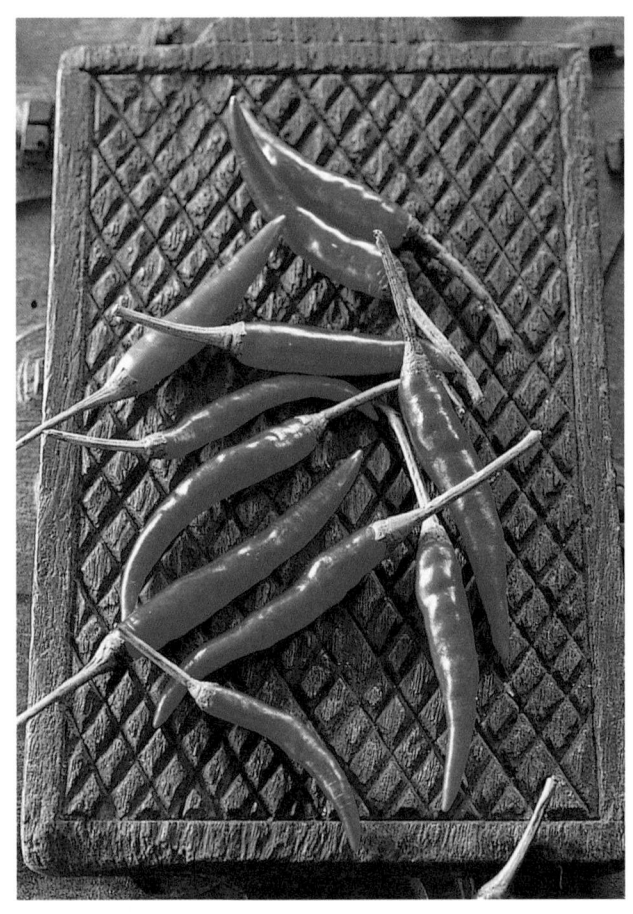

300g Swiss chard *stalks removed*

2 tablespoons virgin olive oil

1 small onion *finely chopped*

20g fresh chorizo sausage (or another spicy sausage) *finely diced*

400g baby new potatoes *cooked and halved*

125g sunblush tomatoes *roughly chopped*

50g Monterey Jack cheese (or mature Cheddar) *grated*

sea salt

spicy mexican potatoes

These are simply a variation of the Spanish *patatas bravas*.

1 Wash the Swiss chard and place in a pan with only the water that clings to the leaves. Cook for 5 minutes over a very low heat, then remove and leave to cool. Roughly chop the leaves.

2 Heat the olive oil in a large non-stick frying pan on a high heat. Add the onion and chorizo and fry until the onion is golden and the oil has been released from the chorizo.

3 Add the potatoes to the pan and fry until golden all over, taking care not to let the onion burn. Add the tomatoes and chopped chard, and cook all together for a further 3–4 minutes, until the flavours are amalgamated. Add the cheese and remove from the heat immediately.

4 Season with a little salt, to taste, then serve.

pg tip Monterey Jack cheese, from California, is one of the few distinctively American cheeses; it is usually known simply as 'Jack cheese'. A mild cheese made from cow's milk, its consistency ranges from soft to hard, depending on the cheese's maturity. It is often used in Latin dishes, such as *quesadillas* and these spicy potatoes.

8 large, very fresh oysters

1 tablespoon virgin olive oil

2 merguez sausages (or fresh chorizo)
cut into 5mm slices

½ small onion *finely chopped*

1 small garlic clove *crushed*

40g cooked spinach

1 tablespoon HP brown sauce

sea salt and freshly ground black pepper

1 tablespoon fresh white breadcrumbs

2 tablespoons Monterey Jack cheese (or
mature Cheddar) *grated*

20g unsalted butter *melted*

lemon wedges, to garnish

barbecue oysters

Barbecuing oysters is a real treat. Furthermore, with the spicy sauce quickly glazed under a rich cheese crust, this is a nice way to enjoy oysters for those who don't like them in their raw, natural state.

1 Shuck the oysters, retaining the shells, and wash thoroughly to remove any grit. Dry well.
2 Preheat the grill to its highest setting.
3 Heat the olive oil in a non-stick frying pan. When hot, add the merguez, onion and garlic and fry until golden in colour, about 5 minutes.
4 Chop the spinach, add this to the pan and cook for a further minute. Add the brown sauce, heat through and season to taste.
5 Place a little of the mixture in the base of each oyster shell and top each with a cleaned oyster.
6 Mix together the breadcrumbs, cheese and melted butter, and spoon over the oysters. Carefully transfer the oysters onto a baking tray and place under the preheated grill. Cook for 3–4 minutes, until the oysters are cooked and the crust bubbling and golden. Garnish with lemon wedges and serve.

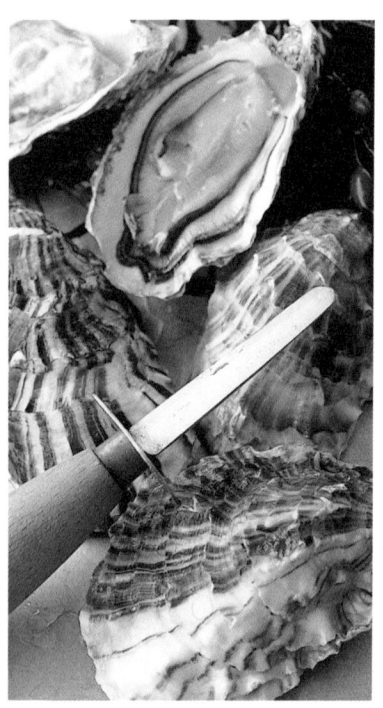

2 tablespoons brown sugar
200g maize flour
2 eggs
120g blue cheese, e.g. Roquefort or Gorgonzola
vegetable oil, for shallow-frying

for the pico
3 ripe, firm plum tomatoes *cut into small dice*
1 clove garlic *crushed*
juice of 2 limes
1 tablespoon maple syrup
2 tablespoons freshly chopped coriander
1 shallot *finely chopped*
sea salt and freshly ground black pepper

arepas with blue cheese pico

Arepas are basically a type of South American corn cake; if you can't find any maize flour, use a fine polenta instead. The blue cheese pico is my take on the classic Mexican salsa *pico de gallo*, whose essential ingredients are tomatoes, chilli and coriander.

1 Heat 350ml water in a small pan with the sugar and stir until dissolved. Sprinkle in the flour a little at a time and beat until you have a smooth, thick dough. Beat the eggs into the dough, one at a time, then beat in half the cheese. Leave to cool.
2 For the pico, mix all the ingredients together in a bowl and season to taste.
3 Roll lumps of the cooled dough in the palm of your hands to form small balls. Flatten the balls gently, then fry them in hot oil in a non-stick frying pan until golden, about 4–5 minutes each side.
4 Transfer the arepas to a serving dish. Crumble the remaining cheese on top and spoon over the pico dressing.

4 tablespoons virgin olive oil
1 tablespoon sherry vinegar
sea salt and freshly ground black pepper
2 x 120g tins sardines, preserved in oil *drained*
2 spring onions *chopped*
2 small roasted red peppers *chopped*
1 red chilli *deseeded and finely chopped*
½ teaspoon smoked paprika
4 slices sourdough bread

smoky sardine sandwich

Okay, so this is a toasted sarnie! But it's a simple comforting sandwich that you'll love to make again and again.

1 Prepare a dressing from the olive oil and vinegar, plus a little salt and pepper.
2 Place the sardines in a single layer in a dish, then scatter over the onions, roasted peppers and chilli. Season liberally with salt, pepper and smoked paprika, then pour over the dressing. Cover with clingfilm and place in the fridge for 2 hours to marinate.
3 When ready to serve, toast the bread slices, then top two of them with the sardines and vegetables. Pour over a little of the marinading juices, then top each with the second bread slice to form a sandwich. Press down lightly to compact the filling.
4 Cut each sandwich into four wedges before serving.

for the dough
300ml prepared chicken stock
150g plain flour

for the filling
2 tablespoons vegetable oil
½ small onion *finely chopped*
1 garlic clove *crushed*
200g minced chicken
2 tablespoons cream cheese
2 tablespoons freshly snipped chives
sea salt and freshly ground black pepper
1 large egg white *lightly beaten*
50g fresh white breadcrumbs
extra vegetable oil, for deep-frying

coxinha

These chicken dumplings (*coxinha* literally means 'little thighs' in Portuguese) are popular all over Brazil.

1 Bring the stock to the boil, sprinkle in the flour, then stir vigorously with a wooden spoon until amalgamated and thick and smooth in consistency.

2 Remove the dough from the pan, allow it to cool a little, then knead until smooth and elastic.

3 For the filling, heat the oil in a non-stick frying pan, add the onion and garlic and cook for 2 minutes until softened. Add the chicken and 2 tablespoons of water, then cook with a lid on for 5–6 minutes, until the chicken is cooked through. Transfer to a bowl and leave to cool. Add the cream cheese and chives, and season to taste.

4 Roll out the dough to about 3mm thick, then cut out 7.5cm circles with a cookie cutter (the dough may be re-used and re-rolled).

5 To make the dumplings, take a circle of dough in the palm of your hand, fill it with the cream cheese mixture, then simply close up the dough.

6 Dip the dumplings in the beaten egg white, then in the breadcrumbs, then fry in hot oil at 150°C/300°F for 4–5 minutes, until golden. Drain on kitchen paper and serve.

pg tip These dumplings freeze well, but they need at least 2–3 hours to defrost completely prior to deep-frying.

8 medium-size flat mushrooms *cleaned*
sea salt and freshly ground black pepper
150g Haloumi cheese *cut into 8 slices*

for the chimichurri
2 garlic cloves *crushed*
1 tablespoooon fresh mint leaves
1 tablespoon fresh oregano leaves
a handful of flat-leaf parsley
1 small red chilli *deseeded and finely chopped*
3 tablespoons white wine vinegar
125ml virgin olive oil

grilled chimichurri mushrooms with haloumi

Chimichurri is an Argentinian sauce traditionally served with grilled meats. It is similar, I suppose, to Italian pesto but without the cheese and with the addition of vinegar to give a touch of piquancy. It tastes great with mushrooms.

1 For the chimichurri sauce, put the garlic, herbs, chilli and vinegar in a small blender and blitz to a coarse paste. Using the feeder tube at the top of the blender, drizzle in 120ml of the olive oil to form a thickish sauce.

2 Preheat a grill pan until hot. Brush each mushroom liberally with the chimichurri then place on the grill. Cook until the mushrooms have softened and released their juices. Season to taste then keep warm.

3 Brush the Haloumi slices with the remaining oil and place on the grill for about 2 minutes on each side, until slightly golden and crispy.

4 Place the mushrooms on a serving dish, along with the grilled cheese, and drizzle over any remaining sauce.

1 tablespoon virgin olive oil
½ **small onion** *finely chopped*
½ **small red chilli** *deseeded and finely chopped*
pinch of ground cumin
250g snapper fillet *boned, skinned, cleaned and roughly chopped*
2 tablespoons freshly chopped coriander
½ **ripe firm mango** *cut into small dice*
2 eggs *beaten*
100g Gruyère cheese
350g shortcrust pastry

snapper and mango empanadas

The empanada is really Latin America's answer to our own Cornish pasty. Be as inventive as you like and create your own fillings. This version goes well with a spicy salsa.

1 Heat the olive oil in a non-stick frying pan, add the onion, chilli and cumin, and cook gently for 2–3 minutes. Remove to a bowl and leave to cool.
2 Once the onion is cool, add the chopped fish, coriander, mango and cheese, and bind with one of the beaten eggs. Place in the fridge for 30 minutes.
3 Preheat the oven to 180°C/350°F/gas mark 4.
4 Roll out the pastry to 3mm thick, then cut out rounds using a 7.5cm cookie cutter. Put a spoonful of the fish mixture in the centre of each circle, then brush around the edge with more beaten egg.
5 Fold the pastry over to make a half-moon shape and press the edges together firmly. Brush the top with the remaining egg, place on a baking tray and bake for 12–15 minutes, until golden. Serve warm.

350g very fresh white crabmeat
juice of 2 limes
sea salt and freshly ground black pepper
1 tablespoon coriander seeds *lightly crushed*
2 tablespoons virgin olive oil
1 tablespoon tomato ketchup
dash of Tabasco sauce
1 small red onion *finely sliced*
2 firm ripe tomatoes *skinned, deseeded and chopped*
75g tinned sweetcorn *drained well*
6 basil leaves *chopped*
tortilla chips
25g mature Cheddar cheese *grated*

crab nachos

Nachos, in their simplest form, are tortilla chips covered in melted cheese. These are an altogether much lighter version.

1 As a precaution, sift through the crabmeat to ensure that there is no hidden cartilage or shell. Place in a bowl and pour over the lime juice. Season with sea salt, cover with clingfilm and refrigerate for 1 hour.
2 Preheat the oven to 200°C/400°F/gas mark 6, or preheat the grill.
3 Mix together the coriander seeds, olive oil, tomato ketchup, Tabasco, red onion, tomatoes and sweetcorn. Stir in the crabmeat (drained of any juices), then add the basil. Season to taste.
4 Carefully spoon the crabmeat onto the tortilla chips and place on a baking tray. Sprinkle over the grated cheese and then bake in the oven or place under the grill for 2–3 minutes, until the cheese is golden and bubbling.

1 tablespoon virgin olive oil
1 onion *finely chopped*
1 green chilli *finely chopped*
1 teaspoon ground cumin
150g cooked black beans
1 recipe for Coca dough (see page 44)
100ml hot salsa sauce
2 tablespoons crème fraîche
75g feta cheese *crumbled*
25g mature Cheddar cheese *grated*

picaditas

The Mexicans love their little pizzas, sold on street corners, and they are certainly extremely moreish. Black beans are among my favourite pulses, especially when cooked with onions, chilli and cumin – ingredients that epitomise for me the flavours of Mexico.

1 Preheat the oven to 200°C/400°F/gas mark 6.
2 Heat the olive oil in a pan then add the onion, chilli and cumin, cooking over a low heat until the onion is tender. Add the cooked beans and mix with the onions, crushing the beans lightly. Fry together for 1–2 minutes, then remove from the heat and leave to cool.
3 Roll out the dough to 5mm thick and cut out twelve 7.5cm circles using a cookie cutter. Transfer the pizza bases to a baking sheet.
4 Spread some black beans thickly onto each base, followed by some salsa. Add a dollop of crème fraîche then sprinkle over a little of both cheeses. Use your fingers to crimp the edges to form a sort of pie crust.
5 Place in the oven to bake for 12–14 minutes, until cooked. Serve warm.

400g black potatoes (also known as truffle potatoes) *washed*
1 onion *finely chopped*
5 tablespoons vegetable oil
75g plain flour
1 egg
sea salt and freshly ground black pepper
150g minced beef
3 spring onions *finely chopped*
1 teaspoon cumin seeds
½ teaspoon ground cinnamon
guacamole and small leaves of watercress, to serve

peruvian potato cakes

In Peru, these potato cakes are commonly known as *causa*. You can use normal potatoes for this recipe but the colour will not be so unusual. Vegetarians could replace the meat with roasted peppers, which taste equally delicious.

1 Preheat the oven to 200°C/400°F/gas mark 6.
2 Place the potatoes on a baking tray, bake in the oven for 40–45 minutes or until cooked through, then remove and cool slightly.
3 Fry the onion in 2 tablespoons of the oil until soft, then transfer to a bowl.
4 Peel the warm potatoes with a small knife, then add to the onions and mash them. Add the flour, beat in the egg and season to taste.
5 Heat the frying pan with another 2 tablespoons of oil and fry the minced beef for 6–8 minutes, until well browned all over. Add to the potatoes, along with the spring onions and spices.
6 With dampened hands, shape the mix into small patties or cakes. Heat the remaining oil in a non-stick pan and shallow-fry the potato cakes until golden and crispy, about 3–4 minutes.
7 Serve each cake topped with guacamole and a little watercress.

buljol

300g cod fillet *boned and skinned*
2 tablespoons coarse sea salt
juice of 1 lime
2 shallots *finely chopped*
1 green pepper *halved, deseeded and cut into small dice*
2 plum tomatoes *cut into small dice*
4 tablespoons virgin olive oil
2 hard-boiled eggs *peeled and chopped*
1 tablespoon chopped flat-leaf parsley
1 avocado *stoned and cut into small dice*
sea salt and freshly ground black pepper
lime wedges, to serve

One could use the classic salt cod for this dish, as they do in the Caribbean, however I find it is better to lightly salt your own fresh cod. The result is definitely lighter, and makes a perfect salad for a hot summer's day.

1 Place the cod in a dish, scatter over the sea salt, cover, and leave to marinate at room temperature for 2 hours.
2 When the time's up, rinse the cod under a little running water to remove any excess salt, then dry well in a cloth.
3 Cut the fish into 2.5cm cubes, place in a pan and just cover with cold water. Slowly bring to the boil and simmer for 3–4 minutes. Remove the cod to a bowl using a slotted spoon and leave to cool.
4 Add the remaining ingredients, toss gently together, and then leave to marinate for 1 hour in the fridge for the flavours to infuse.
5 Serve the salad garnished with the lime wedges.

stuffed peppers with creole crab

10g unsalted butter
1 small onion *finely chopped*
1 small red chilli *deseeded and finely chopped*
200g crabmeat (preferably fresh) *picked over*
3 tablespoons double cream
pinch of curry powder
2 tablespoons fresh white breadcrumbs
50g Gouda cheese *grated*
50g fresh pineapple (tinned is fine) *cut into small dice*
1 tablespoon freshly chopped coriander
8 miniature red peppers
sea salt and freshly ground black pepper

A few years ago, it would have been impossible to obtain miniature-size peppers. Now, however, they are easy to find. These small varieties do not always have the flavour of their more mature cousins, but they make a nice dainty boat for the crab filling.

1 Preheat the oven to 180°C/350°F/gas mark 4.
2 Heat the butter in a pan, add the onion and chilli, and cook until light and golden in colour. Add the crabmeat, cream and curry powder, and cook over a low heat until a sauce forms.
3 Stir in the breadcrumbs, cheese, pineapple and fresh coriander, season to taste and then set aside.
4 Cut the tops off each pepper, discard, and carefully scoop out any inner seeds. Using a teaspoon, fill each pepper with some crab mixture.
5 Stand the filled peppers in a baking tin lined with foil and cook for 12–15 minutes, or until the peppers are soft and the crab filling bubbling and golden. Leave to cool slightly before serving.

peruvian salmon and tuna ceviche

250g very fresh raw tuna fillet (sushi quality)

200g very fresh raw salmon fillet

2 white sweet potatoes *peeled and thinly sliced*

2 tablespoons virgin olive oil

pinch of ground cinnamon

sea salt and freshly ground black pepper

2cm piece root ginger *peeled and finely grated*

juice of 4 limes

1 green chilli *deseeded and finely chopped*

pinch of sugar

2 tablespoons freshly chopped coriander leaves

It may sound an odd combination, but in Peru sweet potatoes are often used as an accompaniment to ceviche, especially when it is made with white fish.

1 Roll the tuna and salmon fillets separately in clingfilm and place in the freezer for no more than 30 minutes, to firm them up a little. (This will make them easier to slice later.)

2 Preheat the oven to 200°C/400°F/gas mark 6.

3 Place the potato slices in a bowl and toss with the olive oil, cinnamon, and salt and pepper. Transfer to a roasting tin and roast for 30 minutes, until golden and cooked through. Keep warm.

4 In a bowl, combine the ginger, lime juice, chilli, sugar and coriander. Season to taste.

5 Take the tuna and salmon out of the freezer, and slice into 3mm-thick slices using a sharp knife. Season the fish with salt and pepper, drizzle over the dressing, then leave to stand for 5 minutes. Garnish with the roasted sweet potato slices.

sardine ceviche

12 small to medium size, very fresh sardine fillets

200ml unsweetened coconut cream

2cm piece root ginger *peeled and finely chopped*

juice of 3 limes

1 small red chilli *deseeded and finely chopped*

pinch of sugar

sea salt and freshly ground black pepper

2 firm ripe tomatoes *deseeded and cut into small dice*

2 tablespoons freshly chopped coriander

75g French beans *topped and tailed*

This ceviche is inspired by the flavours of the Caribbean. Chillies, limes and coconut make the perfect marinade for the rich, oily sardines.

1 Rinse the sardine fillets under cold running water to clean them thoroughly, then pat dry with a cloth.

2 In a bowl, whisk together the coconut cream, ginger, lime juice, chilli and sugar. Season to taste, then add the diced tomatoes and coriander.

3 Lay the sardines in a shallow dish, in a single layer, and pour over the coconut dressing. Cover with clingfilm and marinate in the fridge overnight.

4 When ready to serve, cook the French beans in boiling salted water for 4–5 minutes or until just tender; drain and refresh under cold water, then dry well.

5 Season the beans and divide between serving plates. Top with the marinated sardines and pour over the dressing.

6 very fresh large raw scallops *shelled and cleaned*

½ ripe avocado (preferably Hass variety) *stoned*

½ firm ripe mango *peeled and stoned*

¼ red pepper

juice of 2 limes

1 tablespoon virgin olive oil

pinch of caster sugar

1 small red chilli *deseeded and finely chopped*

2 spring onions *finely shredded*

1 tablespoon chopped chives

sea salt and freshly ground black pepper

scallop ceviche

Scallops are, alongside mussels, perhaps my favourite shellfish to eat and cook with, although they can be quite expensive. You must ensure complete freshness for the ceviche: do not be tempted to use the cheaper frozen ones.

1 Cut each raw scallop horizontally into five thin slices and arrange on serving plates, overlapping the slices to form a circle.

2 Cut the avocado, mango and pepper into small dice and place in a bowl. Add the remaining ingredients.

3 Season the scallops with sea salt and a little pepper, spoon over the dressing, then simply leave to marinate for 5 minutes before serving.

pg tip Hass avocados, which are the main variety grown in the US and New Zealand, have a dark, mottled skin and an unbeatably rich flavour: true guacamole is made from Hass avocados. For the best flavour I find that the avocados should be generally overripe when purchased.

8 medium-size, very fresh mackerel
fillets *boned and cleaned*
1 garlic clove *crushed*
1 small green chilli *chopped*
2 spring onions *chopped*
a handful of fresh coriander leaves
1 small green pepper *deseeded and cut
in pieces*
juice of 4 limes
good pinch of sugar
sea salt and freshly ground black pepper

to serve
1 avocado *halved, stoned and thinly
sliced*
2 tablespoons chopped chives (or chive
shoots)

ceviche verde

For me, mackerel is one of the most underrated and under-utilised fish in
Britain, despite being one of the most plentiful. Its delicate flavour makes
mackerel the ideal vehicle for this green ceviche.

1 Slice the mackerel fillets thinly and place in a shallow serving dish.
2 In a blender, blitz together the garlic, chilli, spring onions and coriander leaves
   until they form a paste; if necessary, use a rubber spatula to push the mixture
   down the sides of the blender.
3 Add the green pepper and blitz again. Add the lime juice and sugar, and quickly
   blitz again. Season to taste. Pour the mixture over the mackerel and leave for
   30 minutes to infuse.
4 Serve garnished with the sliced avocado and chives.

4 tablespoons virgin olive oil
½ teaspoon chilli oil
2 tablespoons lime juice
2 spring onions
¼ cucumber *peeled and seeds removed*
1 red pepper *deseeded*
4 shallots *peeled*
1 tablespoon Vietnamese mint *roughly
chopped*
1 tablespoon Thai basil *roughly chopped*
12 medium-size oysters *shucked and
cleaned on the half shell*

asian-inspired oyster ceviche

You may need to make a trip to your nearest Asian store to pick up the herbs for
this dish, but I promise you won't be disappointed. It's just not the same made
with regular mint and basil.

1 Combine the olive and chilli oils in a bowl. Add the lime juice and mix well.
2 Finely chop the spring onions and cut the red pepper and cucumber into small
   dice; thinly slice the shallots.
3 Add the vegetables to the oil mixture and leave to infuse for 30 minutes. Then
   add the herbs and the oysters and leave to marinate for 5 minutes.
4 Return one oyster to each cleaned shell and spoon over a little of the marinade.
   Serve immediately.

spain

No one who visits Spain could fail to fall in love with the sociable ritual of tapas, or with the exquisite dishes themselves – whether it's a simple plate of Serrano ham or a salad of octopus or sardines.

2 large red peppers *stems removed*
12 green olives *pitted*
12 fresh anchovies marinated in oil
1 tablespoon virgin olive oil
1 teaspoon chopped oregano
½ teaspoon fennel seeds
¼ teaspoon chilli flakes
50g Manchego cheese *finely grated*

olive, anchovy and pepper banderillas

Banderillas, or skewers, are always a pretty addition to the table. In this recipe, the simple flavour combination brings out a real taste of Spain.

1 Preheat the oven to 220°C/425°F/gas mark 7.
2 Cut each pepper into six, lengthways, and place in a roasting tin. Bake in the oven for 15–20 minutes, until the peppers are cooked and their skin is blistered and blackened. Leave to cool slightly, then carefully peel off the skin, taking care not to damage the flesh.
3 Wrap each olive in an anchovy fillet, then roll each inside a piece of roasted pepper. Thread each roll onto a skewer.
4 Place the skewers onto a baking tray, then drizzle over the oil and scatter on the oregano, fennel seeds and chilli flakes. Finally, sprinkle over the cheese and cook in the oven for 5 minutes, until the cheese is bubbling and golden.
5 Cool slightly before serving.

12 small potatoes *unpeeled but well cleaned*
20g unsalted butter
1 shallot *finely chopped*
1 garlic clove *crushed*
150g tinned snails *drained and coarsely chopped*
50g Serrano ham *chopped*
2 tablespoons chopped flat-leaf parsley
sea salt and freshly ground black pepper

stuffed potatoes with snails and ham

The combination of garlicky snails with ham and potatoes may be unoriginal, but it's a marriage made in heaven.

1 Preheat the oven to 200°C/400°F/gas mark 6.
2 Place the potatoes in a small roasting tin and bake for 30–40 minutes until cooked. Remove (leaving the oven on), and leave to cool.
3 Cut the top off each potato, about 1cm down. Using a melon baller, carefully scoop out the inner flesh of each potato, taking care not to break the outer casing.
4 In a frying pan, heat the butter until it foams, then add the shallots, garlic and snails and cook for 1–2 minutes. Add the ham and parsley, and season to taste.
5 Fill each potato with the mixture, and return to the oven for 5 minutes.

for the dough

175g strong white bread flour

75g fine cornmeal

sea salt

½ teaspoon caster sugar

1 x 7g sachet easy-blend yeast

2 teaspoons virgin olive oil

1 red onion *peeled and diced*

100g pumpkin *skinned and thinly sliced*

1 tablespoon red wine vinegar

2 tablespoons tomato purée

2 roasted red peppers *drained (oil reserved) and cut into 5mm cubes*

coca

Coca is the name of a type of Spanish pizza, traditionally baked in a wooden oven and topped with all manner of delicious things. The smoked paprika gives a wonderful woodsmoke flavour and an authentic Spanish note.

1 Sift the flour into a bowl and add 50g of the cornmeal, the salt, sugar and yeast. Make a well in the centre, pour in 150ml warm water, and bring the ingredients together to form a soft, pliable dough.

2 Turn the dough out onto a floured surface and knead gently for 5–6 minutes. Return the dough to the bowl, cover it with clingfilm, then leave it to rise in a warm place for 1 hour.

3 Preheat the oven to 200°C/400°F/gas mark 6.

4 Sprinkle a large baking sheet with the remaining cornmeal. Roll out the dough to roughly 30 x 20cm, and transfer it to the baking sheet.

5 Heat the olive oil in a pan and cook the onion for 5 minutes, until softened. Add the pumpkin slices, cooking gently for a further 5 minutes, until lightly caramelised. Stir in the red wine vinegar and simmer for 2 minutes.

6 Spread the tomato purée over the dough and top with the onion and pumpkin mix, followed by the roasted peppers. Sprinkle over the smoked paprika.

7 Drizzle on the reserved pepper oil and place in the oven to bake for 12–15 minutes, until golden. Scatter over the Manchego cheese and cook for a further 5 minutes.

300g fresh chorizo sausages

125g plain flour

1 teaspoon easy-blend yeast

1 egg *beaten*

sea salt

vegetable oil, for deep-frying

125ml aïoli (see page 59), to serve

buñuelos

These fritters originated in Spain, but you also find them in Mexico and other parts of Latin America. They are made with a wheat-based dough and are traditionally sweet, but there are savoury versions too – some made with cheese or, as here, spicy chorizo.

1 Cut the sausages into 2cm-thick slices.

2 Make a batter with the flour, yeast, egg and 100ml water. Season with a little salt.

3 Heat the oil to 160°C/325°F.

4 Dip the sausage chunks in the batter then immerse them in the hot oil. Fry until they are golden and crispy, then drain on kitchen paper. Serve with the aïoli.

4 thick slices country bread
2 tablespoons virgin olive oil
120g fresh pineapple *skin removed*
1 teaspoon brown sugar
120g Valdeon cheese *thinly sliced*
8 slices Jabugo ham

jabugo ham with pineapple and valdeon cheese

Jabugo ham tastes sensational and is undoubtedly Spain's greatest ham. It is expensive, however, so you could use Serrano or Parma ham instead for this recipe. Valdeon (also known as Picos de Europa) is a Spanish blue cheese, similar to Roquefort in taste and appearance.

1 Heat a grill pan until very hot. Brush the bread slices with the olive oil and place on the grill to toast on both sides until charred.

2 Cut the pineapple into semi-circles, sprinkle liberally with brown sugar, then place on the grill pan until lightly caramelised. Remove from the heat and cut into small chunks.

3 Top the toasts with the cheese, lay the sliced ham on top, then garnish with the grilled pineapple.

1 teaspoon virgin olive oil
1 small onion *finely chopped*
1 garlic clove *crushed*
150g cooked new potatoes *peeled*
1 x 185g tin tuna in oil *drained*
75g soft goat's cheese
6 green olives *pitted and chopped*
2 teaspoons superfine capers *rinsed and drained*
a little paprika
sea salt and freshly ground black pepper
350g shortcrust pastry
a little beaten egg

tuna and goat's cheese empanadillas

Empanadillas are smaller, pocket-size versions of *empanadas*, and are the ideal party food. Understandably perhaps, they are often associated with South America, but in fact they originated in Spain's northern region of Galicia, where they are still popular.

1 Preheat the oven to 200°C/400°F/gas mark 6.

2 Heat the olive oil in a frying pan over a low heat. Add the onion and garlic and cook for 4–5 minutes, until softened, then remove to a large bowl. Leave to cool.

3 Add the potatoes and lightly crush with a fork. Add the tuna, goat's cheese, olives and capers, mixing gently together. Add the paprika and season to taste.

4 Roll out the pastry on a floured surface to 3mm thick, then cut out 20–25 rounds using a 7.5cm cookie cutter.

5 Place a good spoonful of the mixture in the middle of each pastry circle, brush the edges with egg, then bring up the sides to meet at the top to form a small parcel, pasty style. Crimp the pastry along the top to secure the filling.

6 Brush with some beaten egg and bake on a baking tray for 12–15 minutes, until golden and flaky.

pg tip If you don't want to cook the empanadillas straight away, the uncooked pastry parcels can be kept in the fridge for 1–2 days, or for up to one month in the freezer.

300g squid tubes *cleaned and roughly chopped*
1 small onion *finely chopped*
2 tablespoons chopped flat-leaf parsley
2 tablespoons dry sherry
sea salt and freshly ground black pepper
200g lean minced pork
100g white breadcrumbs
1 egg *beaten*
2 tablespoons virgin olive oil

for the sauce
3 tablespoons virgin olive oil
1 garlic clove *crushed*
good pinch of saffron filaments
2 tablespoons plain flour
180ml prepared fish stock

squid meatballs with saffron

The recipe for these tasty meatballs, which hails from Andalucía, was given to me by a Spanish chef friend of mine. I always found the combination of squid and pork somewhat daunting, but they both have the same glutinous texture and so complement each other well. In Spain, pork is often combined with seafood such as squid, clams, mussels and prawns.

1 Place the chopped squid in a food processor and blitz to a coarse paste. Transfer to a bowl and add the onion, parsley, sherry and seasoning. Refrigerate for 30 minutes.

2 For the sauce, heat the oil with the garlic and saffron for about 1 minute. Stir in the flour and cook for 20 seconds before adding the fish stock. Mix well to form a sauce, simmer for 15 minutes, then strain.

3 Mix the squid with the pork mince, breadcrumbs and egg, and shape into 2.5cm balls.

4 Heat the olive oil in a frying pan. When hot, gently fry the squid balls until golden, about 5–6 minutes.

5 Serve the squid and pork balls with the saffron sauce spooned over – they look lovely presented on small spoons.

2 tablespoons virgin olive oil
1 garlic clove *crushed*
pinch of paprika
sea salt and freshly ground black pepper
16 large raw king prawns *shelled and deveined (tails kept on, heads removed)*

for the mojo verde
1 garlic clove *crushed*
a small handful of coriander, leaves only
a small handful of flat-leaf parsley
1 small green pepper *deseeded and cut into small pieces*
100ml virgin olive oil
2 tablespoons red wine vinegar

prawns a la plancha with mojo verde

Cooking *a la plancha* simply means cooking on a hot grill – a quick and easy way to seal in flavour. The *mojo verde* (green sauce) comes from the Canary Islands, where it is normally served with fish.

1 Mix the olive oil, garlic, paprika and salt and pepper in a dish. Add the prawns, toss well, and leave for 30 minutes to marinate.

2 For the mojo verde, place the garlic, coriander and parsley in a blender and blitz. Add the pepper, olive oil and vinegar and blitz again until smooth. Season to taste.

3 Heat a grill pan and, when very hot, add the prawns and cook for 2–3 minutes, turning occasionally. Serve them hot from the grill with the green sauce.

piperrada

2 tablespoons virgin olive oil
½ **onion** *finely chopped*
1 **garlic clove** *crushed*
1 **small green pepper** *deseeded and cut into 1cm cubes*
1 **small red pepper** *deseeded and cut into 1cm cubes*
2 **firm ripe tomatoes** *cut into 1cm cubes*
4 **eggs** *lightly beaten*
sea salt and freshly ground black pepper
2 **slices country bread** *cut into 1cm cubes*
75g **Serrano ham** *chopped*
1 tablespoon chopped flat-leaf parsley

Egg dishes provide a cheap and nutritious meal and are popular throughout Spain. This omelette-cum-pepper stew recipe comes from the Basque region, and is great for breakfast or brunch.

1 Heat half the olive oil in a frying pan. Add the onion, garlic and peppers and cook for 5–6 minutes, or until the peppers have softened and taken on a little colour. Add the tomatoes and cook for a further 2 minutes.
2 Raise the heat, then pour in the beaten eggs, allowing them to set a little before gently folding them in with the vegetables. Season to taste.
3 Heat the remaining oil in another frying pan and add the bread cubes, ham and parsley. Cook until the bread is lightly golden.
4 Spoon the eggs onto serving dishes and top with the bread mixture.

gazpacho seafood salad

2 **eggs** *hard-boiled and peeled*
2 **ripe firm tomatoes** *chopped*
1 **small onion** *chopped*
1 **small green pepper** *deseeded and cut into 1cm dice*
1 **small red pepper** *deseeded and cut into 1cm dice*
1 **garlic clove** *crushed*
1 tablespoon white wine vinegar
4 tablespoons olive oil
2 tablespoons chopped flat-leaf parsley
1 tablespoon chopped basil
250g **pack cooked seafood selection**
sea salt and freshly ground black pepper

This salad is fresh and extremely appetising. It uses some of Spanish cookery's most typical ingredients to great effect.

1 Cut the eggs in half, remove the cooked yolk, mash it with a fork and place to one side; chop the cooked white.
2 Place the tomatoes, onion, peppers and chopped egg whites in a bowl.
3 Mix the garlic, cooked egg yolk, vinegar and oil to form a dressing. Add the herbs and then stir into the tomato mixture.
4 Finally, throw in the cooked seafood and season to taste.

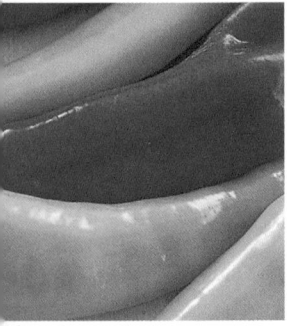

px glazed pork

1 small pork fillet (or sliced pork belly) *cut into 2cm cubes*
1 clove garlic *crushed*
1 teaspoon freshly picked oregano
1 tablespoon olive oil
2 tablespoons vegetable oil
350g baby onions
sea salt and freshly ground black pepper
4 rashers of streaky bacon *roughly chopped*
120ml Pedro Ximénez sherry

I adore Pedro Ximénez sherry in dishes. It is wonderfully sweet and rich, and works really well with pork. The recipe could be made with chicken if you prefer.

1 Marinate the pork in a bowl with the garlic, oregano and olive oil for 1 hour.
2 Heat the vegetable oil in a large non-stick frying pan. When hot, add the onions and fry for 4–5 minutes, until golden. Set aside.
3 Return the pan to the heat, season the pork with salt and pepper and fry in the pan for 4–5 minutes. Add the bacon and cook for a further 2 minutes.
4 Return the onions to the pan, pour over the sherry, and cook with the lid on for 4–5 minutes, until the meat and onions are cooked and the sauce has reduced to a glaze. Transfer to a serving dish and pour over the pan juices.

calamari with chorizo and salsa verde

500g small squid *cleaned*
2 tablespoons virgin olive oil
125g fresh chorizo *thinly sliced*
100g cooked white beans (tinned is fine)

for the salsa verde
2 garlic cloves *crushed*
50g flat-leaf parsley
50g fresh basil leaves
1 anchovy fillet
1 tablespoon superfine capers
1 tablespoon white wine vinegar
4 tablespoons extra virgin olive oil
1 hard-boiled egg *roughly chopped*
sea salt and freshly ground black pepper

Capers and anchovies are the signature ingredients of *salsa verde*, which packs much more of a punch than the *mojo verde* on page 51. It is one of the tastiest of sauces, and goes wonderfully with the calamari, while the chorizo adds a little spice to the dish.

1 To prepare the squid, cut off the fins then pull the bag and the tentacles apart. Remove the backbone and any soft innards from the bag. Cut away the head from the tentacles, and discard. Rinse the squid in cold water and dry in a cloth. Slice thinly and set aside.
2 For the green sauce, place the garlic, herbs and anchovy in a small blender and blitz to a coarse pulp. Add the capers and blitz quickly again. Transfer to a bowl and add the vinegar and oil to form a semi-liquid sauce. Finally, add the egg and season to taste.
3 Heat the olive oil in a large non-stick pan over a high heat, add the chorizo and fry until slightly crispy. Add the squid and cook for a further 2 minutes, still on a high heat.
4 Quickly add the cooked beans and green sauce and toss together. Transfer to a dish and serve immediately.

pg tip Chorizo comes either cooked (and ready-to-eat) or uncooked. The latter, which is the only type used in this book, is normally sold as a string of small sausages, which you can slice up and add to all manner of savoury dishes.

600g **large plump mussels** *cleaned and debearded*

1 **bottle Spanish beer (or another light beer)**

6 **rashers streaky bacon**

2 **eggs** *beaten*

100g **white breadcrumbs**

1 **tablespoon virgin olive oil**

50g **unsalted butter**

2 **tablespoons chopped flat-leaf parsley**

sea salt and freshly ground black pepper

mussels with bacon and cerveza

When preparing this dish, try to find the largest, plumpest mussels available: wrapping up a tiny mussel in bacon would be a very fiddly job!

1 Place the mussels in a hot pan over a high heat. Pour over the beer, cover quickly with a lid and cook until the mussels open, about 2–3 minutes. Remove from the heat and strain, reserving the cooking liquor. Leave the mussels to cool.

2 Remove the cold mussels from their shells. Cut the bacon rashers in half and wrap each half around one mussel.

3 Dip the mussel parcels in the beaten egg, then in the breadcrumbs. Thread them equally onto four presoaked bamboo skewers.

4 Heat the olive oil with half the butter in a frying pan and cook the skewers for 2–3 minutes on each side, until golden. Transfer to a serving plate.

5 Add the reserved mussel juices and the remaining butter to the pan, and boil together for 1 minute. Sprinkle in the chopped parsley and then pour around the skewered mussels to serve.

pg tip Remember to discard any mussels that are open when purchased, as these are dead, and again discard any that remain closed once they have been cooked.

chorizo with sweet melon and mint

100g sweet Ogen (green-fleshed) melon
*peeled, deseeded and cut into 1cm
cubes*
100g sweet Cantaloupe or Charentais
(orange-fleshed) melon
50g watermelon
1 tablespoon virgin olive oil
300g good-quality fresh chorizo *thickly
sliced*
120ml dry sherry
sea salt and freshly ground black pepper
2 tablespoons freshly chopped mint

I just love the way the spicy and sweet pair together in this dish. It's a
real winner.

1 Heat the olive oil in a large frying pan and fry the chorizo slices until they are
brown and crisp on the outside but still juicy within. (The chorizo yields plenty
of its own fat, so don't overdo the olive oil.)
2 Add the melon pieces, quickly toss together, then pour over the sherry. Let it
bubble up for 30 seconds. Add 2 tablespoons of water and cook for another
minute. Season with a touch of salt and black pepper.
3 Transfer to a serving dish and sprinkle over the mint.

boquerones with soft-cooked eggs and aïoli

3 tablespoons virgin olive oil
juice of ½ lemon
1 tablespoon white wine vinegar
2 small garlic cloves *thinly sliced*
sea salt and freshly ground black pepper
300g fresh anchovies *cleaned*
4 eggs
1 tablespoon freshly chopped flat-leaf
parsley

for the aïoli
150ml good-quality mayonnaise
2 garlic cloves *crushed*

Boquerones are small fresh anchovies from Spain. They are delicious marinated,
particularly when smothered with the yolk oozing out of soft-boiled eggs.

1 Prepare the marinade by mixing the oil, lemon juice, vinegar, garlic and salt
and pepper.
2 Fillet the anchovies with a small knife, then lay the fillets in a dish. Pour over
the marinade, cover, and leave for 4 hours.
3 Make the aïoli by mixing the mayonnaise and garlic together in a bowl.
4 When ready to serve, soft boil the eggs in a large pan of simmering water,
for 3–4 minutes. Remove with a slotted spoon and run under cold water for
30 seconds to cool the eggs sufficiently for you to peel them.
5 Arrange the eggs in a serving dish, garnished with the marinated anchovies.
Sprinkle over the parsley and serve with the garlic mayonnaise alongside.

pg tip The best way to fillet a fresh anchovy is to simply pull the head of each
anchovy firmly down through the belly and towards the tail. This releases the
spine, leaving the fish split in a butterfly fashion.

300g **fresh squid** *cleaned and tentacles removed*

2 tablespoons **virgin olive oil**

1 **onion** *finely chopped*

2 **garlic cloves** *crushed*

1 teaspoon **smoked paprika**

150g **paella or risotto rice**

800ml **fish stock**

3 sachets **squid ink**

1 **lemon** *cut into wedges, to serve*

for the saffron allioli

pinch of **saffron filaments (soaked in boiling water)**

1 **garlic clove** *crushed*

100ml **good-quality mayonnaise**

black paella

Don't be put off by the sound of the squid ink used in this recipe (it adds a little saltiness and works with the rice to great effect), nor by the fish stock: excellent fresh stocks are available in good supermarkets these days. The *allioli* is simply a Catalan version of aïoli (garlic mayonnaise).

1 Cut the squid into rings. Heat half the olive oil in a heavy-based pan until very hot. Add the squid and cook for 1 minute until sealed all over. (If you cook the squid for any longer it will turn rubbery.) Set aside.

2 Add the onion and garlic to the pan, along with the remaining olive oil and the paprika, and cook gently for 1–2 minutes. Add the rice and stir until it is well coated with the oil, onion and spice.

3 Heat up the fish stock in a pan, add the squid ink, then pour this over the rice. Lower the heat to barely a simmer and cook for 15–18 minutes, until nearly all the liquid has been absorbed and the rice is al dente. Return the squid to the rice and mix well.

4 For the allioli, mix the saffron and garlic into the mayonnaise, stir well and serve with the paella, along with lemon wedges.

2 **little gem lettuces** *leaves separated, washed, dried and torn into small pieces*

2 **sticks of celery** *thinly sliced*

4 **spring onions** *shredded*

100g **good-quality cooked ham** *cut into strips*

2 **roasted red peppers in oil** *drained and chopped*

2 slices **country bread** *toasted and cut into small cubes*

50g **Manchego cheese** *finely grated*

for the dressing

5 **marinated fresh anchovies**

100ml **mayonnaise**

1 **garlic clove** *crushed*

1 tablespoon **red wine vinegar**

dash of **Worcestershire sauce**

sea salt and freshly ground black pepper

spanish caesar salad

A simple play on the classic Caesar salad, loved the world over.

1 In a bowl, mix the ingredients for the dressing together, and season to taste.

2 In another bowl, toss together the lettuce, celery, spring onions, ham, peppers and toasted bread. Pour over the dressing and toss well.

3 Arrange the salad on serving plates and sprinkle over the Manchego cheese.

mushroom and artichoke escabeche

Escabeche is a Spanish term for food (usually fish or vegetables) that is lightly soused or pickled. This dish is ideal for vegetarians.

100ml virgin olive oil

2 shallots *thinly sliced*

good pinch of saffron filaments (or ½ teaspoon powdered variety)

300g chestnut or button mushrooms *halved (or, if large, quartered)*

2 tablespoons white wine vinegar (or rice wine vinegar)

1 tablespoon caster sugar

1 teaspoon crushed coriander seeds

½ teaspoon black peppercorns *lightly cracked*

1 small bay leaf

1 small jar artichoke halves in oil *drained (reserving the oil)*

1 tablespoon flat-leaf parsley leaves

1 Heat the oil in a frying pan over a low heat, add the shallots and saffron, and fry for 4–5 minutes, until the shallots begin to caramelise to a light golden brown.

2 Add the mushrooms and cook for a further 5–6 minutes, or until the mushrooms are brown and just cooked through.

3 Add the vinegar, sugar, coriander seeds, peppercorns, bay leaf and 100ml water. Cover with a lid and simmer for 8 minutes.

4 Remove the lid, add the artichoke halves plus a little of the oil from the jar, cover again and cook for a further 5 minutes.

5 Remove from the heat, transfer to a dish, and leave to cool to room temperature. Scatter over the parsley leaves before serving.

spanish-style bruschetta

A Spanish version of the classic Italian bruschetta – a contradiction in terms, perhaps, but delicious all the same. Vegetables work beautifully in this recipe, and fish such as sardines and anchovies would go well, too.

1 green pepper *deseeded and cut into thick strips*

1 red pepper *deseeded and cut into thick strips*

1 small aubergine *cut into 1cm cubes*

2 garlic cloves *crushed*

1 teaspoon oregano *chopped*

100ml olive oil

2 tablespoons sherry vinegar

pinch of sugar

4 slices sourdough bread

1 large very ripe and juicy tomato

sea salt

Manchego shavings, to serve

1 Preheat the oven to 200°C/400°F/gas mark 6.

2 Place the peppers, aubergine cubes and half the crushed garlic in a roasting tin. Scatter over the oregano and drizzle over half the oil, then place in the oven for 25–30 minutes, until the vegetables are charred and cooked through.

3 Transfer the vegetables to a bowl and add the vinegar and sugar. Leave to marinate for 2 hours.

4 To serve, heat the remaining olive oil in a large non-stick frying pan and fry the slices of bread until golden and crisp. Remove from the pan and smear on the remaining crushed garlic.

5 Next, squeeze and crush the tomato over the surface of the bread, and sprinkle with sea salt.

6 Arrange the vegetables neatly on the tomato toasts, drizzle over any juices and place the cheese shavings on top.

1 tablespoon virgin olive oil
1 shallot *finely chopped*
16–20 fresh razor clams
sea salt and freshly ground black pepper

for the romesco
2 dried red peppers *deseeded and soaked in water for 1 hour*
100ml virgin olive oil
1 red chilli *chopped*
3 garlic cloves *crushed*
1 slice white bread *cut into 2.5cm pieces*
3 tablespoons blanched almonds *toasted*
1 tablespoon tomato purée
2 tablespoons white wine vinegar
sea salt

razor clams with romesco sauce

Razor clams are not always readily available, but you should be able to order them from your fishmonger. It's worth it, they are delicious! Eat them grilled just with lemon and olive oil, or as they are here, topped with one of Spain's greatest sauces, *romesco*.

1 For the romesco, first drain and dry the peppers, then chop finely. Heat half the olive oil in a frying pan and fry the peppers and fresh chilli, taking care not to burn them. Set aside. In the same oil, fry the garlic and bread until golden, then set aside.

2 Place the almonds and tomato purée in a blender, along with the pepper and bread mixtures, and blitz to a smooth paste. Add the remaining oil and vinegar, and season with salt.

3 When ready to serve, heat the olive oil in a frying pan with the shallot, cook for 1–2 minutes, then add the clams. Pour over 100ml water, cover with a lid, and cook until the shells open, about 2 minutes.

4 Transfer the clams to a serving dish, add the sauce to the cooking juices in the pan and adjust the seasoning. Pour the sauce over the clams to serve.

pg tip Dried peppers – traditionally mild nora chilli peppers from Spain – are the most important ingredient in romesco sauce. You can find them in good delis, but if you need to substitute, you could use ¼ teaspoon of chilli flakes.

50g plain flour
¼ teaspoon baking powder
3 spring onions *finely chopped*
2 tablespoons chopped flat-leaf parsley
250g peeled brown shrimps or small prawns
sea salt and freshly ground black pepper
a little paprika
vegetable oil, for frying

crispy shrimp pancakes

This is an unusual dish of tiny brown shrimps crisply fried in a light onion and parsley batter, which I first tasted in a tapas bar in Alicante, southern Spain. The generous sprinkling of sea salt before serving is essential.

1 Place the flour and baking powder in a bowl, add 90ml water and stir to a smooth batter.
2 Add the spring onions, parsley and shrimps, and season with salt, pepper and paprika. Leave to stand, covered, for 1 hour in the fridge.
3 Pour enough vegetable oil in the bottom of a frying pan to reach a depth of 1cm, and put on the heat. When the oil is hot, add spoonfuls of batter and fry until golden, turning the pancakes over with a palette knife to cook both sides.
4 Drain the pancakes on kitchen paper and sprinkle liberally with sea salt.

375g new potatoes *unpeeled*
1 onion *finely chopped*
2 garlic cloves *crushed*
2 tablespoons sherry vinegar
150ml virgin olive oil
1 x 185g tin of tuna in oil *drained*
2 tablespoons chopped flat-leaf parsley
sea salt and freshly ground black pepper
garlic bread *to serve*

tuna and potato salad

I rarely open a tin of anything as a rule, but for this salad 'dip' preserved tuna works best. Just make sure you buy the best quality you can find.

1 Place the potatoes in a pan of boiling salted water and cook for 15–20 minutes. Drain in a colander and allow the potatoes to cool enough for you to peel them comfortably.
2 Place the potatoes in a food processor, add the onion, garlic, vinegar, half the oil and half the tuna, and blitz to a paste.
3 With the motor running, drizzle in the remaining oil through the feeder tube at the top of the processor, to form a smooth purée.
4 Transfer to a serving dish, scatter over the remaining tuna, sprinkle on the parsley and season. Serve at room temperature with slices of crisp garlic bread.

400g waxy potatoes, peeled
75ml virgin olive oil
1 onion *very thinly sliced*
2 garlic cloves *crushed*
6 large eggs
sea salt and freshly ground black pepper

mini potato tortillas

Although a common dish, tortilla is easy to make badly. The key to this recipe is making sure that you leave the potatoes to soak properly in the egg mixture (softening them in the process). You could, of course, use a small frying pan if you don't possess any small tart tins.

1 Slice the potatoes very thinly using a mandolin slicer or a sharp knife. Dry them on kitchen paper.
2 Heat the olive oil in a large non-stick frying pan over medium heat. Throw in the potato slices, onion and garlic and cook for 15–20 minutes, or until the potatoes are tender and the onions lightly caramelised.
3 Beat the eggs in a bowl with a generous sprinkle of salt and pepper. Gently stir the potatoes into the eggs and set aside for 10–15 minutes.
4 Preheat the oven to 180°C/350°F/gas mark 4.
5 Lightly oil eight 7cm tart tins all over (Yorkshire pudding or muffin tins will do if necessary), then fill with the egg and potato mix.
6 Place on a baking sheet and cook for 12–15 minutes, or until just set. Loosen the tortillas, then remove, or alternatively eat them from the tins.

pg tip You can add some chorizo to the onion to give these tortillas an extra touch of heat. They are great eaten hot or cold, and taste good with garlic mayonnaise.

chilled oysters with cava granita

550ml cava (or sparkling wine)
¼ small cucumber *halved lengthways then thinly sliced*
pinch of sea salt
12 oysters *shucked and cleaned*
10g caviar (optional luxury)

Here's a sexy dish if ever there was one: cool, briny oysters, cucumber and caviar, all offset with iced cava shavings. This dish is one big treat for the taste buds!

1 Mix 300ml water with the cava in a small shallow container and place in the freezer. Put the cucumber and salt into a bowl to extract excess water.
2 After 30 minutes, remove the emerging cava granita from the freezer and mix it around with a fork to break up the granules. Return it to the freezer for 2 hours, stirring occasionally.
3 Remove the oysters from their shells. Wash and dry the shells, reserving enough for each oyster to be served on the half shell.
4 Place a bed of cucumber in each half shell, then top with an oyster.
5 Break up the granita again, then spoon some onto each oyster. Top with the caviar, if using. Eat in one mouthful for the ultimate experience.

seafood escabeche

75g sunblush tomatoes in oil *drained*
1 head of fennel *peeled and cut into 1cm wedges*
1 garlic clove *sliced*
1 small bay leaf
2 tablespoons virgin olive oil
sea salt and freshly ground black pepper
100ml water
50ml white wine vinegar
100ml dry white wine
200g baby clams
350g mussels
175g baby squid *tentacles removed and cleaned*

The word *escabeche* is thought to have originated in Persia, where it was used to describe a dish of poached or fried fish served with its acidic marinade. You'll find a similar dish elsewhere, too, including the *escovitch* of Jamaica and the *scapece* of Italy.

1 Preheat the oven to 180°C/350°F/gas mark 4.
2 Place the vegetables, garlic and bay leaf in a roasting tin or casserole. Pour on half the olive oil and toss well. Season with salt and pepper, then place in the oven to cook for 30 minutes, until lightly caramelised.
3 Bring the water, wine vinegar and white wine, plus a little sea salt, to the boil. Add the seafood, drizzle over the remaining oil, and cook with a lid on for 1–2 minutes, until the seafood is cooked. Remove from the heat and leave to cool.
4 Arrange the vegetables in a shallow dish, followed by the seafood. Spoon over some of the poaching liquid and top with freshly ground black pepper.

europe

Small plates in Europe range from the antipasti of Italy to the *amuses-bouche* of France and the *smorgasbord* of Sweden. They share a respect for fresh ingredients and an emphasis on harmonious flavour combinations.

russian omelette

10g unsalted butter

2 small onions *thinly sliced*

250g new potatoes *boiled, peeled and thickly sliced*

¼ teaspoon dill seeds

8 eggs

125ml double cream

sea salt and freshly ground black pepper

225g smoked salmon *diced*

sour cream

fresh dill, to garnish

a little caviar (optional)

Why Russian you say? I wanted to include an egg-based dish with smoked salmon… smoked salmon led me to caviar (why not?) … and that led to sour cream… and then the dish suddenly became obvious.

1 Melt the butter in a 25cm non-stick frying pan or omelette pan, add the onions and cook on a low heat until golden, about 5–6 minutes. Add the cooked potatoes and dill seeds.

2 Preheat the grill to a moderate heat.

3 Beat the eggs in a bowl, add the double cream, and season to taste with salt and pepper. Pour half the eggs into the pan and scatter the smoked salmon on top. Cook for a few minutes or until the omelette begins to set, then pour over the remaining eggs and cook for a further 5–6 minutes.

4 Remove from the heat and place under the preheated grill until the omelette rises and browns.

5 Transfer the omelette to a board and cut into wedges. Serve with sour cream and a scattering of fresh dill. For a taste of real luxury, you could add a dollop of caviar in between.

star anise-cured salmon

8 star anise pods

3 tablespoons caster sugar

3 tablespoons sea salt

500g very fresh thick salmon fillets, skinless

2 lemons *very thinly sliced*

for the dipping sauce

150ml good-quality mayonnaise

1 cooked beetroot *chopped*

½ teaspoon Dijon mustard

1 teaspoon runny honey

I first came across the pairing of star anise with salmon in Stockholm. Here, it is ground up and added to salt and sugar to form the cure for a gravadlax-style marinade.

1 Place the star anise pods in a mortar, or in a small coffee grinder, and crush to a fine powder. Add the sugar and salt, then rub the mixture over the salmon fillets.

2 Top the salmon with the lemon slices, then wrap tightly in foil. Place on a tray in the fridge to marinate overnight.

3 For the dipping sauce, place all the ingredients in a blender and blitz to a smooth sauce. Season to taste.

4 Take the salmon out of the fridge, remove the lemon slices, and scrape off any remaining spice mixture. Slice the fillet into 5mm-thick slices, arrange on a dish and serve with the dipping sauce.

pg tip For an alternative presentation for this recipe, you could cut the cured salmon into cubes and thread it on to wooden skewers.

110g unsalted butter
150g plain flour *sifted*
4 eggs *beaten*
150g Stilton cheese
100g Gruyère cheese
sea salt and freshly ground black pepper
vegetable oil, for deep-frying

stilton fritters

Stilton cheese is one of Britain's greatest treasures. These little fritters are a great way to use up any trimmings or small pieces left from a cheese board.

1 Bring 300ml water to the boil. Add the butter, then quickly sprinkle in the flour and beat with a wooden spoon until the mixture leaves the side of the pan. Remove from the heat.

2 Beat the eggs into the mixture in three stages, beating well each time. Then, while the mixture is still warm, beat in the cheeses. Season well.

3 Heat the oil in a pan to 160°C/325°F. Fry the fritters in batches, dropping spoonfuls of the batter into the hot oil and cooking until golden.

4 Drain on kitchen paper then serve.

pg tip These Stilton fritters taste delicious with plum chutney, or even apple or a good tomato chutney. Vegetable or beetroot pickles would make a good accompaniment, too.

1 large aubergine
1 garlic clove *peeled and thinly sliced*
6 tablespoons virgin olive oil
1 small onion *finely chopped*
1 small red pepper *chopped*
½ small green pepper *chopped*
2 ripe firm tomatoes *deseeded and chopped*
½ teaspoon sugar
juice of ¼ lemon
sea salt and freshly black ground pepper

ikra

This Russian aubergine salad is equally good served as a spread; simply blitz it in the blender at the final stage. In Russia, the traditional accompaniment is dark rye or pumpernickel bread.

1 Preheat the oven to 220°C/425°F/gas mark 7.

2 Using a small knife, pierce holes randomly into the aubergines and fill the holes with the thinly sliced garlic.

3 Rub some olive oil over the aubergine and place on a baking tray. Bake in the oven for 1 hour, turning occasionally, until the aubergine is charred and blistered.

4 Meanwhile, heat 3 tablespoons of the oil in a pan, add the onion and cook for 5–6 minutes until softened. Add the peppers, cook for a further 5 minutes until softened, then transfer to a bowl.

5 Remove the skin carefully from the aubergine, then chop the pulp finely until almost a purée. Add this to the pepper mixture.

6 Stir in the tomatoes, sugar, lemon juice and remaining olive oil. Season with salt and pepper.

black pudding, apple and bacon pies

1 tablespoon vegetable oil
1 small onion *finely chopped*
½ teaspoon freshly picked thyme
2 rashers back bacon *chopped*
2 tablespoons raisins *soaked in water until plump, drained*
1 Granny Smith apple *peeled, cored and chopped*
170g black pudding
sea salt and freshly ground black pepper
300g shortcrust pastry
a little beaten egg

Whenever I serve these little pies alongside drinks, they seem to disappear in no time. I suggest you prepare them in bulk, as you're bound to eat more than you think, and they also freeze well.

1 Heat the oil in a frying pan. When hot, add the onion and thyme and cook for 5–6 minutes, until the onions are softened.

2 Raise the heat, add the bacon, raisins and apple, and fry until the bacon is cooked and the apple caramelised. Finally, add the black pudding. Mix well together and cook until the mixture is well mashed up. Season to taste, remove from the heat and leave to cool.

3 Preheat the oven to 200°C/400°F/gas mark 6. Lightly oil 12–15 small tartlet moulds (a mini muffin tin is also fine).

4 Roll out the pastry to 3mm thick, then cut out twelve circles using a 6cm cutter. Cut out another twelve circles, using a 5cm cutter, for the tops.

5 Line the moulds with the larger pastry circles, then add a spoonful of the black pudding mix. Brush around the edges of the pastry with the beaten egg before toppping each pie with a smaller pastry round. Press down gently to seal and brush with the remaining egg.

6 Using a small knife, make a couple of slits in the top of each pie, then bake for 12–15 minutes, until golden. Allow to stand for a moment or two before removing from the mould and serving.

quail's eggs with smoked and spiced sea salt

12 quail's eggs
2 tablespoons coarse sea salt
1 tablespoon freshly chopped chives
¼ teaspoon smoked paprika

Quail's eggs have suddenly become trendy, and are widely available. They have a delicate, almost gamey flavour and taste wonderful either soft or hard-boiled.

1 Bring a pan of water to the boil, carefully immerse the quail's eggs and reduce the heat to a simmer. Cook the eggs for 4 minutes, then remove and immediately refresh in iced water.

2 Carefully peel the eggs and place on individual spoons or, alternatively, pile them in a bowl.

3 Mix the sea salt, chives and paprika, sprinkle a little on each egg and serve.

pg tip Other ways to serve quail's eggs include: with celery salt, to dip in anchovy-flavoured mayonnaise, or simply with caviar for a gastronomic treat.

300g mushrooms of your choice (e.g.
portabello, chestnut, shiitake, oyster or
trompettes)

3 tablespoons virgin olive oil

2 garlic cloves *crushed*

sea salt and freshly ground black pepper

1 ball buffalo mozzarella *thinly sliced*

2 small ciabatta rolls *halved horizontally*

1 teaspoon freshly picked thyme leaves

oven-roasted mushrooms with mozzarella bread

Roasting the mushrooms with a little garlic and thyme really brings out their flavour. If you can't find an interesting selection of mushrooms, choose a single favourite variety instead.

1 Preheat the oven to 220°C/425°F/gas mark 7.

2 Clean the mushrooms, slice thickly, then place in a roasting tin. Spoon over 2 tablespoons of the olive oil, add the garlic, season with salt and pepper, and mix well. Place the mushrooms in the hot oven to roast for 15–20 minutes, until golden and tender.

3 Meanwhile, lay overlapping slices of mozzarella onto the ciabatta halves, drizzle over some of the remaining olive oil and sprinkle over the thyme. Place on a baking tray and bake until golden and crispy and the cheese is melting.

4 To serve, cut the ciabatta into thick fingers and arrange around the mushrooms in a serving dish.

europe

2 tablespoons virgin olive oil
4 salted anchovy fillets *rinsed, dried and finely chopped*
1 garlic clove *crushed*
2 tablespoons crushed walnuts
1 tablespoon white wine vinegar
40g unsalted butter
zest of ½ lemon
2 tablespoons chopped flat-leaf parsley
40g fresh white breadcrumbs *lightly toasted*
16 green asparagus tips
sea salt

asparagus with toasted anchovy gremolata

The classic Italian gremolata consists simply of garlic, parsley and grated lemon. The addition of some anchovy and walnuts makes a fantastic topping for the lightly poached asparagus. And try adding an oozingly soft poached egg to the dish, too – delicious!

1 Heat the olive oil in a non-stick frying pan, add the anchovies and heat until softened. Add the garlic and walnuts and cook for 1 minute, then pour over the vinegar.
2 Add the butter to the pan and wait for it to start foaming before adding the lemon zest, parsley and breadcrumbs. Keep warm.
3 Cook the asparagus tips in boiling salted water for 2–3 minutes, then drain.
4 Arrange the asparagus on a dish and scatter over the gremolata.

2 tablespoons virgin olive oil
1 garlic clove *crushed*
375g small courgettes *cut at an angle into 1cm slices*
30ml red wine vinegar
30ml honey
25g currants
sea salt and freshly ground black pepper
1 teaspoon superfine capers *well rinsed*
3 tablespoons flaked almonds *toasted*

sweet and sour courgettes

The Italians really know how to cook vegetables, and make them taste out of this world. Here's a simple dish I first encountered in Venice.

1 Heat the oil in a large frying pan, add the garlic and fry over a medium heat until the garlic is just beginning to colour.
2 Throw in the courgette slices and cook for 3–4 minutes, until lightly coloured all over. Pour on the vinegar and honey, then add the currants.
3 Cover the pan with a lid and cook for 4–5 minutes, stirring occasionally.
4 Transfer the courgettes to a dish, to be served either warm or at room temperature. Before serving, season to taste, add the capers and scatter over the flaked almonds.

12 large cherry tomatoes

1 teaspoon caster sugar

1 garlic clove *crushed*

½ teaspoon freshly picked oregano leaves

sea salt and freshly ground black pepper

virgin olive oil

325g puff pastry

120g firm, matured goat's cheese *diced*

1 small pear *peeled and thinly shaved, to serve*

for the black oil

6 tablespoons virgin olive oil

8 black olives

goat's cheese tarts with black oil

The slow roasting of the little tomatoes really brings out their natural sweetness and accentuates their flavour.

1 Preheat the oven to 220°C/425°F/gas mark 7.

2 Cut the cherry tomatoes in half and arrange on a foil-lined baking sheet. Sprinkle them with the sugar, garlic, oregano, some salt and a drizzle of olive oil.

3 Place in the oven to slow roast for 30 minutes, by which time the tomatoes should be soft and wilted but not mushy. Remove from the oven and leave to cool.

4 To make the black oil, simply blend the olive oil and olives in a small blender until the olives are finely chopped.

5 Roll out the pastry to 3mm thick, then cut out twelve 7.5cm circles using a fluted cookie cutter. Prick each pastry circle with a fork and top with roasted tomatoes (cut side up).

6 Transfer to a baking tray and place in the oven for 8–10 minutes, until the tarts are nearly cooked. Scatter over the diced goat's cheese and return to the oven for a further 2 minutes.

7 Remove and leave to cool. Before serving, drizzle with the black oil and top with shavings of the thinly sliced pear.

400g **pork belly** *cut into 5cm pieces*
125g **pork back fat** *cut into 5cm pieces*
150ml **dry white wine**
2 **garlic cloves**
1 **bay leaf**
4 **sprigs of thyme**
pinch of **mace**
sea salt and freshly ground black pepper
a little **flour**
2 **eggs** *beaten*
100g **white breadcrumbs**
vegetable oil, for frying

for the sauce
100ml **vinaigrette dressing**
1 chopped tablespoon each of: **capers,
gherkins, shallot, hard-boiled egg and
flat-leaf parsley**

crispy pork rillettes

Pork rillettes are one of the triumphs of classic French cookery, and are simple to prepare, if a little time-consuming. If time is of the essence, you could buy the rillettes from a deli; just make sure that they are of excellent quality.

1 Preheat the oven to 150°C/300°F/gas mark 2.
2 Mix together all the ingredients for the rillettes (from pork belly down to salt and pepper) in a heavy-based casserole. Cover with a tight-fitting lid and cook in the oven for 3–4 hours, or until the meat is falling apart. Leave to cool. Remove the bay leaf and thyme.
3 Lift the pork meat out of the pan and roughly shred using two forks. Return the meat to the pork fat and pan juices, and season to taste. Pack into a small terrine or loaf tin and leave overnight in the fridge.
4 Remove the rillettes from the terrine and cut into roughly 1cm cubes. Dip in the flour, the egg and then in the breadcrumbs.
5 Heat the oil in a frying pan and fry the breaded cubes until golden and crispy.
6 Make the sauce by mixing all the ingredients together and serve with the crispy rillettes.

1 **large jar preserved baby artichokes**
2 **garlic cloves** *crushed*
a handful of **fresh basil leaves**
2 tablespoons **freshly grated Parmesan**
1 tablespoon **pine nuts**
pinch of **sugar**
sea salt and freshly ground black pepper
juice of ½ lemon

artichokes in their own sauce

I first created artichoke pesto some years ago, as part of a pasta dish for a competition. It evolved into a sauce to serve with marinated artichokes – a surprising combination that has proved very popular among both vegetarians and meat-eaters.

1 Drain the artichokes, reserving the oil. Place a quarter of them in a small blender and blitz to a coarse purée. Add the garlic, basil, Parmesan, pine nuts and sugar, and blitz again.
2 With the motor running, drizzle in the artichoke oil through the feeder tube to form a pesto-like sauce. Season and add lemon juice to taste.
3 Place the remaining artichokes on a serving dish, pour over the artichoke sauce and serve.

500g very fresh halibut fillet *skinned and boned*

juice of 1 lemon

4 tablespoons virgin olive oil

sea salt and freshly ground black pepper

½ small red chilli *deseeded and finely chopped*

2 ripe firm tomatoes *deseeded and cut into small dice*

8 fresh basil leaves *roughly chopped*

6 black olives *pitted and chopped into small pieces*

1 teaspoon superfine capers *rinsed and dried*

3 red radishes *very thinly sliced*

halibut crudo

In Italy, fish or meat served *crudo* (i.e. 'raw') is becoming as popular as ceviche in Mexico. I particularly love fish prepared in this way. The important thing to remember is that the fish must be super-fresh.

1 Using a thin and very sharp knife, cut the halibut fillet into 3mm-thick slices. Place in a shallow dish and season well with salt and pepper.

2 In a bowl, whisk together the lemon juice and olive oil with some salt and pepper. Add the remaining ingredients, mix well, and pour over the halibut. Cover and leave to marinate in the fridge for 30 minutes.

3 Serve the fish slices with the delicious marinade poured over the top.

2 tablespoons virgin olive oil

1 head fennel *very thinly sliced*

½ teaspoon fennel seeds

100g smoked salmon *diced*

2 tablespoons fresh dill *chopped*

sea salt and freshly ground black pepper

2 tablespoons cream cheese

for the blinis (makes 12–16)

50g buckwheat flour

25g plain flour

½ teaspoon baking powder

1 egg *beaten*

120ml buttermilk or milk

20g unsalted butter *melted*

extra butter, for frying

salmon tartare on blinis

A great and classic appetiser, salmon tartare is also a good way to use up any trimmings of smoked salmon.

1 To make the batter for the blinis, sift the flours into a bowl, add the baking powder, then stir in the egg, buttermilk (or milk) and melted butter. Stir until smooth then leave to rest for 15 minutes.

2 Heat the oil in a pan, add the fennel and fennel seeds, and cook over low heat for 15–20 minutes, until tender and caramelised.

3 Place the salmon in a bowl, add the dill, salt and pepper.

4 Melt about half a tablespoon of butter in a small non-stick frying pan. Drop tablespoons of batter into the pan in batches, cooking the blinis until golden on each side. Remove and keep warm.

5 To serve, place a little of the fennel mixture on each blini, followed by a dollop of cream cheese, and top with the salmon.

goat's cheese in provençal oil

4 firm goat's cheeses (or one log cut into 4 sections)

60g sunblush tomatoes in oil *drained*

1 teaspoon black peppercorns

4 garlic cloves *peeled and thinly sliced*

4 small bay leaves

4 sprigs rosemary

4 sprigs thyme

4 fresh or dried lavender sprigs

150ml virgin olive oil

Quite recently, I started giving these goat's cheeses in oil to guests as soon as they arrived in my restaurant, to whet their appetite. They have been a great success, and guests regularly ask for more as a starter to their meal. Thin slices of toasted walnut bread go superbly with the melting cheese, but warm baguette or focaccia bread are good, too.

1 Place each goat's cheese inside a small preserving jar. Divide the tomatoes, spices and herbs equally between the four jars, then add a sprig of lavender to each jar, too. Cover each cheese with olive oil.

2 Seal down the lids and keep refrigerated for one week prior to use.

3 When ready to serve, preheat the oven to 120°C/250°F/gas mark ½. Place the jars in a roasting tin with 2.5cm of water in the bottom and heat in the oven for 30 minutes, after which time the cheese should be warm and slightly softened in texture.

4 Let your guests enjoy eating the cheese straight from the jars.

chilli-roasted fries with sour cream

4 large floury potatoes (Desirée or Maris Piper)

100ml virgin olive oil

sea salt

1–2 teaspoons chilli powder (or to taste)

sour cream, to serve

Here's a dish of simplicity if ever there was one. The potatoes can be replaced with sweet potatoes for a nice change.

1 Preheat the oven to 220°C/425°F/gas mark 7.

2 Cut each potato into eight wedges and place in a bowl. Add the olive oil, salt and chilli powder, and toss until evenly coated.

3 Transfer to a baking sheet, cook for 15–20 minutes, turn them over and cook for a further 15–20 minutes. Turn the potatoes again and continue cooking for a final 20 minutes, turning them until crisp and golden.

4 Cool slightly before serving with a dip of sour cream.

devilled whitebait

400g fresh whitebait
sea salt and freshly ground black pepper
vegetable oil, for deep-frying
4 tablespoons milk
2 tablespoons plain flour
cayenne pepper
lemon wedges, to serve

I am so pleased to include this recipe in the book. These crispy little fishes, lightly devil-spiced with cayenne pepper, were one of the first dishes I ever prepared as a trainee chef at catering college many years ago.

1 Rinse the whitebait in cold water, drain and dry well. Season the fish with salt and pepper.
2 Heat the vegetable oil to 160°C/325°F.
3 Dip the fish into the milk, drain, dip straight into the flour, then fry until golden and crispy; this should take only 1–2 minutes. Drain on crumpled newspaper or kitchen paper.
4 Dust lightly with cayenne pepper, garnish with lemon wedges and serve.

pg tip Crumpling up kitchen paper before using it to drain fried food allows the oil to be drained off more thoroughly. Newspaper works just as well as kitchen paper.

stuffed sardines with celery-leaf pesto

8 medium-size fresh sardines *cleaned*
2 tablespoons virgin olive oil

for the stuffing
1 tablespoon virgin olive oil
50g fresh white breadcrumbs
2 tablespoons raisins *soaked in water for 20 minutes, dried and chopped*
2 hard-boiled eggs *chopped*
sea salt and freshly ground black pepper

for the pesto
50g celery leaf (as green as possible)
25g flat-leaf parsley
1 garlic clove *crushed*
30g pine nuts *lightly toasted*
100ml virgin olive oil

Celery leaves usually get banished to the cheese tray, as garnish, or thrown into a stock or sauce. What a waste! Use them to create this unusual pesto to serve with sardines.

1 Preheat the oven to 200°C/400°F/gas mark 6.
2 For the stuffing, heat the olive oil in a non-stick frying pan, add the breadcrumbs and fry until lightly golden in colour. Transfer to a bowl and leave to cool. Add the raisins, eggs and season to taste.
3 Cut the heads off the sardines, open them up by slitting along the belly with a knife, and carefully remove the inner spines. Wash the inside and pat dry.
4 Stuff the sardines with the stuffing, pressing the sides together, then place in a baking dish. Season with salt and pepper, drizzle over the remaining oil, then bake in the hot oven for 10–12 minutes.
5 Meanwhile blitz the celery leaf, parsley, garlic and pine nuts in a blender. Add the olive oil to form a light sauce, and season to taste.
6 Transfer the sardines to a serving dish, drizzle over the pesto and serve.

12 cherry tomatoes *stems removed*

1 tablespoon tapenade

12 *bocconcini* (baby mozzarella)

½ teaspoon grated lemon zest

2 tablespoons virgin olive oil

1 tablespoon chopped flat-leaf parsley

cherry tomato and bocconcini lollipops

A simple but eye-catching recipe based on the Caprese salad, Italy's ubiquitous pairing of mozzarella and tomato.

1 With a sharp knife, remove the top 1cm of each tomato. Using a melon baller, scoop out the seeds of each one, ensuring that the outer 'shell' is left intact.

2 Spoon a little tapenade into the base of each tomato, followed by one of the baby *bocconcini*.

3 Skewer the base of each tomato with a large wooden or bamboo skewer. For the most eye-catching presentation, stand the lollipops in tall glasses.

4 In a bowl, combine the lemon zest, olive oil and parsley. Drizzle a little over each tomato before serving.

50g unsalted butter

175g plain flour (plus a little extra for rolling)

425ml milk

2 tablespoons virgin olive oil

200g fresh porcini mushrooms (or any cultivated mushroom) *roughly chopped*

1 large shallot *finely chopped*

1 small garlic clove *crushed*

sea salt and freshly ground black pepper

2 eggs *beaten*

125g dry white breadcrumbs

200ml virgin olive oil, for deep-frying

porcini croquettes

Porcini (or cep) are a variety of *Boletus* mushroom. The name originates from the Latin word *bolet*, meaning 'superior mushroom', which is exactly what porcini are. They have a distinct aroma, reminiscent of fermented dough.

1 Firstly, melt the butter in a pan, sprinkle in the flour and beat until smooth, cooking over a low heat to form a classic roux. Add the milk a little at a time, ensuring each addition is combined with the roux before adding more. Cook over a low heat for 5–8 minutes until the sauce is smooth, satin-like in appearance and very thick in consistency. Set aside.

2 Heat the olive oil in a frying pan. When hot, add the roughly chopped mushrooms and cook for 2–3 minutes, until they are tender and golden. Add the shallot and garlic and cook for a further 2 minutes.

3 Add the mushroom mix to the white sauce, stir well, season to taste and then transfer to a bowl to cool. Once cooled, transfer the mixture onto a lightly floured surface and shape into a long roll approximately 2cm in diameter. Cut into 3cm sections.

4 Coat each formed croquette with the egg and breadcrumbs. (These uncooked croquettes can be chilled until needed.)

5 When ready to serve, heat the olive oil to 160°C/325°F in a deep frying pan and fry the croquettes a few at a time for 2–3 minutes, until heated through and golden.

4 slices Parma ham *halved*

8 small sage leaves (plus extra, to garnish)

2 tablespoons *mostarda di Cremona* (Italian mustard fruits), *chopped*

350g monkfish fillet *skinned, boned and cut into 8 cubes*

sea salt and freshly ground black pepper

3 tablespoons virgin olive oil

30g unsalted butter

zest of ½ lemon

1 teaspoon balsamic vinegar

monkfish spiedini with mustard fruits

A *spiedino* is the name of a kebab in Italian. The idea to use Parma ham and sage to wrap up the monkfish parcel comes from the classic Italian dish *saltimbocca*, though this traditionally uses veal rather than fish.

1 Lay out the halved Parma ham slices on a work surface. In the centre of each, place a sage leaf, a little mustard fruit and, lastly, a cube of monkfish. Season lightly with salt and pepper. Wrap the ham around the fish to form parcels, securing each with a cocktail stick or skewer.

2 Heat 2 tablespoons olive oil in a frying pan. When hot, add the parcels and fry for 2–3 minutes on each side, until golden and tender. Remove and keep warm on a serving dish.

3 Clean the pan with kitchen paper and return to the heat. Add the butter and heat until it foams up, then add the lemon zest and the vinegar. Let the sauce bubble for 30 seconds.

4 Heat the remaining 1 tablespoon of olive oil in a pan, and fry a handful of sage leaves for about 30 seconds, until crisp. Drain on kitchen paper.

5 Pour the sauce over the fish parcels, scatter over the fried sage leaves and serve immediately.

pg tip Italian mustard fruits, known in Italy as *mostarda di Cremona* or *mostarda di frutta*, are candied fruits preserved in a sweet, mustard-flavoured syrup. They go beautifully with sausages, cold meats and cheese. You'll find them in Italian delis.

12 **Medjool dates** *pitted*
50g **Gorgonzola cheese** *lightly crumbled*
6 **rashers of streaky bacon**

for the polenta squares
100g **quick-cook polenta**
25g **unsalted butter**
2 **tablespoons grated Parmesan**
2 **tablespoons virgin olive oil**

piggyback dates on polenta

Medjool dates are the best dates you can buy: sweet, sticky, out of this world…
In contrast, the bacon and cheese add some necessary saltiness, making one
hell of a canapé.

1 To prepare the polenta squares, bring 700ml water to the boil in a pan and
then gradually add the polenta, stirring constantly until it acquires a porridge-
like consistency. Reduce the heat to low and cook for 10–12 minutes, until the
polenta is very thick.
2 Add the Parmesan and butter, then spread into a shallow, well-greased 20cm
baking tray. Refrigerate overnight, covered in clingfilm.
3 The next day, cut the dates lengthways across the top, without cutting right
through. Open them up as far as you can. Fill each date with Gorgonzola, then
wrap in half a rasher of bacon, spearing each with a cocktail stick.
4 Heat a grill pan until very hot and brush with olive oil.
5 Cut the polenta into twelve 5cm diamonds. Place on the grill and cook until
golden on both sides. At the same time, grill the dates until the bacon is crispy.
6 Serve the dates on top of the grilled polenta diamonds.

300g **fresh chicken livers** *(frozen livers
are fine but must be fully defrosted)*
100ml **milk**
3 **tablespoons virgin olive oil**
sea salt and freshly ground black pepper
¼ **teaspoon fennel seeds**
4 **tablespoons balsamic vinegar**
4 **ripe but firm figs** *cut into wedges*
8 **slices French bread** *(or sourdough)*

chicken liver bruschetta with balsamic figs

Figs and balsamic vinegar work so well together, and the combination of the
sweet fruit and tart vinegar is the perfect foil for the rich chicken livers. A little
rocket goes nicely with this dish, adding an extra peppery bite.

1 Cut the liver into bite-size pieces, remove any traces of green bile, then place
in a bowl. Pour over the milk and leave to soak for 30 minutes (this helps to
remove any bitterness).
2 Remove the livers from the milk, quickly rinse in cold water, then dry them well.
3 Heat the olive oil in a non-stick frying pan. Once the oil is hot, season the livers
with salt, pepper and the fennel seeds, and add to the pan. Fry over a high heat
for about 1 minute.
4 Pour over the vinegar and let it bubble for a while. Add the figs and toss with
the liver pieces until they are all well coated in glaze (making sure that the livers
stay pink in the centre).
5 To serve, toast the bread slices until golden, pile the glazed livers on top, and
drizzle over any remaining pan juices.

225g plain flour
pinch of salt
1 x 7g sachet easy-blend yeast
8 salted anchovy fillets *halved, rinsed and dried*
50g Gorgonzola cheese *crumbled*
vegetable oil, for frying

zeppole with anchovy and gorgonzola

These doughnut-like pastries, eaten mainly in Calabria and other parts of southern Italy, are normally filled with a sweet cream. This version, however, is savoury, made with one of Italy's greatest cheeses.

1 Sift the flour into a bowl. Add the salt and yeast, then make a well in the centre. Pour in 150ml warm water and bring the ingredients together to form a soft, pliable dough. Place in a lightly oiled bowl, cover with clingfilm, and leave in the fridge for 2 hours.

2 Transfer the dough to a work surface and knock it back for about a minute.

3 Divide the dough into 16 small balls. Flatten each one on the palm of your hand, place a piece of anchovy and some Gorgonzola in the centre, and fold over the dough to secure the filling. Flatten lightly with the other hand, stretching the dough as you do so.

4 Heat a frying pan with 2.5cm oil in the bottom. When hot, cook the *zeppole* in batches until golden. Drain on kitchen paper and serve.

120ml virgin olive oil
500g pork belly *cut into small cubes*
1 tablespoon smoked paprika
2 onions *peeled and chopped*
1 garlic clove *crushed*
75g streaky bacon *cut into small dice*
3 red peppers *deseeded and cut into strips*
3 firm tomatoes *blanched, peeled and deseeded*
1 tablespoon freshly chopped flat-leaf parsley
1 tablespoon freshly chopped coriander
1 small red chilli *finely chopped*
400g clams or cockles

cataplana

Many of you may have eaten this pork and shellfish stew while on holiday in Portugal. The word *cataplana* is actually the name of the dish that the stew is cooked and served in. But, never fear, a flameproof casserole will do the job fine.

1 Heat the olive oil in a heavy-based casserole. When hot, add the pork and paprika and fry for 5–6 minutes, until the meat is crispy all over.

2 Add the onions, garlic, bacon and peppers and sauté for a further 5 minutes. Then add the tomatoes, herbs and chilli. Reduce the heat and allow to cook gently with a lid on for 5–6 minutes.

3 Finally, add the clams, mix well and cook with the lid on over a low heat for 5 minutes. Transfer to deep soup bowls to serve.

¼ **small cucumber** *deseeded and cut into small pieces*
1 **small red onion** *thinly sliced*
2 **tomatoes** *cut into small pieces*
½ **teaspoon dried oregano**
2 **tablespoons red wine vinegar**
4 **tablespoons virgin olive oil**
75g **feta cheese**
1 **garlic clove** *crushed*
8 **black olives** *stoned and finely chopped*
4 **pitta breads**
125g **Cheddar cheese**

greek-style quesadillas

Feta cheese, the key ingredient in this simple recipe, is a great cheese to serve as an appetiser, its saltiness working wonders with an apéritif.

1 In a bowl, combine the cucumber, onion, tomatoes, oregano, vinegar and 2 tablespoons of the olive oil. Leave to stand for 20 minutes, then drain thoroughly.

2 Crush the feta cheese in a bowl with the garlic and olives. Cut the pittas in half, horizontally, then spread the insides of four halves with the feta mixture.

3 Divide the salad over these four halves, sprinkle over the Cheddar, then cover with the remaining pitta halves to form sandwiches.

4 Heat the remaining oil in a large non-stick frying pan over a moderate heat, and cook the 'quesadillas' until the cheese melts, about 2–3 minutes per side. Cut into wedges to serve.

pg tip Always choose a good-quality feta, which traditionally is a blend of 30 per cent goat's milk and 70 per cent sheep's milk. Beware of the cheap, poorly produced versions on the market.

north africa
and the middle east

From Turkey to Tunisia, mezze are one of the most enchanting traditions of this region – a glorious array of little dishes that can start or make a meal.

1 onion *peeled and cut into quarters*
good pinch of saffron filaments
400g cooked chickpeas (the tinned variety is fine), *drained*
75g tahini
½ teaspoon ground cumin
pinch of cayenne pepper
2 garlic cloves *crushed*
sea salt and freshly ground black pepper
2 tablespoons virgin olive oil

moroccan-style hummus

In my opinion, there's no better way to prepare hummus. It's such a great dip, and a wonderful spread for vegetarian sandwiches.

1 Place the onion in a small pan with the saffron and 2 tablespoons of water. Cover with a lid and cook gently for 10 minutes, until the onion is tender. Drain into a colander and leave to cool.

2 Place the onion and all the remaining ingredients (except the olive oil) in a blender or food processor and blitz to a smooth purée, adding a little more water if necessary. Season to taste.

3 Transfer to a serving dish, drizzle over the olive oil and serve with lots of toasted Middle Eastern-style flatbread.

1 teaspoon caraway seeds
½ teaspoon cumin seeds
400g freshly ground lamb mince
1 onion *grated*
1 garlic clove *crushed*
½ teaspoon paprika
2 tablespoons freshly chopped mint
6 black olives *pitted and finely chopped*

for the sauce
75g blanched almonds
1 slice white bread *cut into small pieces*
3 tablespoons virgin olive oil
good pinch of saffron filaments
1 tablespoon tahini
750ml chicken stock
2 tablespoons vegetable oil

turkish lamb kofta in tchina sauce

The sauce served with these spicy lamb meatballs is simply the African version of tahini.

1 You need to prepare the koftas the day before you plan to eat them.

2 Place a small dry frying pan on a high heat, add the caraway and cumin seeds, and toast until fragrant, about 15 seconds. Shake the pan constantly to prevent the spices from burning. Place in a spice blender or mortar and crush to a fine powder.

3 Transfer the crushed spices to a bowl, then add the lamb and the remaining kofta ingredients. Mix well but do not overwork.

4 Using wet hands, divide the mixture into small balls about 2.5cm in diameter. Refrigerate overnight on a plate, covered with clingfilm.

5 To make the sauce, fry the almonds and bread pieces in the olive oil until golden in colour. Remove to a blender or food processor, add the saffron, tahini and 185ml of the chicken stock, and blitz to a smooth sauce.

6 Heat the oil in a flameproof casserole, add the meatballs and seal all over, until golden. Add the saffron sauce and remaining stock, bring to the boil, and simmer very gently for 20 minutes, until the meatballs are cooked through. Thin the sauce with a little water if necessary.

7 Transfer the kofta to a serving dish and pour over the sauce.

300g lean minced beef or lamb
50g cooked rice
sea salt and freshly ground black pepper
1 small onion *finely chopped*
2 tablespoons chopped flat-leaf parsley
½ teaspoon dried mint
1 teaspoon ground cardamom
1 tablespoon natural yoghurt
1 teaspoon virgin olive oil
2 eggs
a little flour
50g unsalted butter

kadin budu

These twice-cooked meatballs are popular throughout Syria. The recipe, particularly the type of meat, varies from town to town: some prefer lamb, others beef.

1 Place the meat in a bowl with the rice, seasoning, onion, parsley, dried mint, cardamom, yoghurt, olive oil and one of the eggs. Mix together to form a smooth paste.

2 Using wet hands, divide the mixture into around 20–25 balls the size of a small golf ball, then flatten each one a little in the palm of your hand.

3 Place the meatballs in a pan and just cover with boiling water. Reduce the heat to a simmer and cook for 10 minutes. Drain and leave to cool.

4 Beat the remaining egg, dip the meatballs in it, then roll them in the flour. Heat the butter in a frying pan, add the balls and fry until crisp and brown.

75g fresh spinach leaves *cooked and chopped*
1 red chilli *deseeded and finely chopped*
1 garlic clove *crushed*
zest of ½ lemon
200g cooked chickpeas *mashed with a fork*
225g chickpea flour (gram flour)
1 teaspoon baking powder
75g feta cheese *grated*
3 eggs
a handful of fresh coriander leaves *chopped*
vegetable oil, for deep-frying

for the beetroot tzatziki
60g cooked beetroot *finely chopped or grated*
4 tablespoons natural yoghurt
1 tablespoon freshly chopped mint

chickpea and spinach fritters with beetroot tzatziki

These light and fluffy fritters are beautifully simple to make, and nutritious, too. The beetroot tzatziki adds a touch of elegance alongside.

1 Put all the ingredients for the fritters (excluding the oil) in a bowl. Mix together well, then leave to chill for 1 hour in the fridge.

2 For the tzatziki, mix the ingredients together in a bowl and season to taste.

3 Heat the oil in a large frying pan to 160°C/325°F. Drop in walnut-sized spoonfuls of the fritter mixture, and fry until golden.

4 Drain on kitchen paper and serve immediately with the beetroot tzatziki.

400g chicken thighs *skinned, boned and cut into 2.5cm pieces*
sea salt and freshly ground black pepper
1 tablespoon paprika
2 garlic cloves *crushed*
4 tablespoons natural yoghurt
juice of ½ lemon
2 tablespoons vegetable oil
2 flour tortillas
4 tablespoons garlic mayonnaise (see aïoli recipe on page 59)
½ small red onion *finely sliced*
1 firm ripe tomato *roughly chopped*

shish taouk wraps

There are as many marinade recipes as there are cooks. Here's one of the simplest and one of my favourites, inspired by Lebanon's *shish taouk*, grilled garlic chicken. The yoghurt really tenderises the meat beautifully, while the garlic and paprika add an all-encompassing flavour.

1 Place the thigh pieces in a bowl and season well with salt and pepper. Add the paprika, garlic, yoghurt and lemon juice, and mix together well. Cover with clingfilm and refrigerate overnight.

2 To serve, remove the chicken from the marinade and dry off any excess. Thread the pieces onto four barbecue skewers.

3 Heat a grill pan and brush it liberally with oil. Cook the skewers on the grill for 6–8 minutes, turning them regularly until cooked and lightly charred.

4 Place the flour tortillas on the grill for 1 minute on each side to reheat them.

5 Spread a little garlic mayonnaise onto each tortilla, add some meat down the centre, and then top off with some onion and tomato. Wrap the tortilla tightly to secure the filling. Cut each tortilla in half to serve.

pg tip Paprika as a seasoning seems to be making a culinary comeback. There are some great ones available, Hungarian probably being the most sought after. Spanish paprika is good, too, including *picante pimentón*, Spain's wonderful smoked paprika.

lebanese chicken wings

100ml virgin olive oil

good handful of coriander, leaves only

juice of 2½ lemons

2 garlic cloves *crushed*

2 tablespoons maple syrup

1 teaspoon ground cumin

½ teaspoon ground coriander

¼ teaspoon ground cayenne pepper

½ teaspoon sumac

12 large chicken wings

2 tablespoons vegetable oil

Chicken wings are very cheap, and really do make a good tidbit for canapés and the like. Most butchers now sell them due to the growing demand.

1 In a blender, combine the olive oil, coriander, juice of 2 lemons, garlic, maple syrup, dried spices and sumac, and blitz until smooth. Transfer to a bowl.

2 Make three slashes in the meaty part of each chicken wing, add to the marinade and toss well. Marinate for 4 hours at room temperature.

3 Preheat a ridged grill pan. Meanwhile, thread the wings onto four wooden or bamboo skewers, reserving the marinade. Brush the wings with vegetable oil, place on the very hot grill and cook for 4–5 minutes, or until the wings are crispy and caramelised in appearance. Baste the chicken with the reserved marinade occasionally as they cook.

4 Transfer to a serving dish and squeeze over the juice from the last half lemon.

4 x 100g fresh salmon trout fillets, skin on
sea salt
smoked paprika

for the chermoula
4 tablespoons virgin olive oil
good pinch of powdered saffron (or turmeric)
1 garlic clove *crushed*
½ teaspoon ground cumin
2 tablespoons freshly chopped mint
1 tablespoon flat-leaf parsley
juice of 1 lemon
sea salt and freshly ground black pepper

paprika salmon trout with mint chermoula

I love the colours in this dish – they are amazingly appealing to both the eye and the palate. Salmon is fine if you can't get hold of the trout.

1 Make several slashes across the skin of the salmon trout fillets. Season them liberally with salt and smoked paprika, using your hands to push the seasoning into the cut slats in the fish. Leave to marinate for 1 hour.

2 Meanwhile, make the chermoula. Place the olive oil and saffron together in a small pan over a low heat for 5–8 minutes. Remove and leave to cool.

3 Mix the remaining chermoula ingredients in a bowl, add the saffron oil and season to taste.

4 Grill the fish on a preheated hot grill for 3–4 minutes on each side. Coat with the chermoula and serve.

75g fresh white breadcrumbs
12 small chicken drumsticks *skinned*
1 tablespoon Dijon mustard
a little plain flour
2 egg whites *lightly beaten*

for the dukkah
25g nibbed almonds
20g sesame seeds
15g coriander seeds
5g cumin seeds
sea salt and freshly ground black pepper

dukkah-crumbed drumsticks

Dukkah is an Egyptian spice mix that is simply delicious. The more you eat the more addictive it becomes. Sprinkle it on crusty bread drizzled with olive oil, or use it to coat chicken, as in this recipe. If you're wondering what to serve with the drumsticks, small crisp French fries fit the bill perfectly.

1 For the *dukkah*, heat a dry frying pan and, when hot, add the almonds and seeds. Toast for 30 seconds, stirring all the time. Crush in a mortar with some salt and pepper, but not too finely. Mix the *dukkah* with the breadcrumbs.

2 Brush the drumsticks liberally with the mustard. Dip them in the flour, in the beaten egg whites and then, finally, in the *dukkah* crumb mix.

3 Preheat the oven to 200°C/400°F/gas mark 6.

4 Place the chicken drumsticks in a single layer on a baking tray and bake for 15–20 minutes, or until cooked and golden.

175g frozen peas

375g chickpeas *soaked in cold water overnight*

2 spring onions *finely chopped*

1 garlic clove *crushed*

1 teaspoon ground cumin

1 red chilli *deseeded and finely chopped*

2 tablespoons freshly chopped mint

50g white breadcrumbs

1 egg

sea salt and freshly ground black pepper

2 tablespoons vegetable oil

pea and mint tameyas

Tameyas are, essentially, a type of Israeli falafel. The inclusion of peas gives a wonderful colour and freshness to the patties. Chilli-spiked yoghurt would make a nice accompaniment.

1 Blanch the peas in boiling water for 1 minute, then drain well.

2 Drain the chickpeas thoroughly and process in a food processor with the peas and remaining ingredients (except the oil) until smooth. Season to taste.

3 Roll the mixture into golf ball-size balls, flatten them into patties and place on a tray. Cover and refrigerate for 1 hour.

4 When ready to serve, heat the oil in a frying pan and fry the patties until golden, 1–2 minutes per side. Drain on kitchen paper.

100ml virgin olive oil

1 onion *finely chopped*

1 garlic clove *crushed*

2 x 170g chicken breasts *skinned, boned and minced*

a little cinnamon

½ teaspoon sugar

pinch of saffron filaments

60g raisins

50g peeled pistachios (optional)

1 packet filo pastry (or spring roll pastry)

1 egg *beaten*

a little icing sugar

chicken briouats

These crispy stuffed filo parcels, which usually come in a triangle or cigar shape, are one of the most popular street foods in Morocco. The light sprinkling of icing sugar at the end is in keeping with the Moroccan penchant for adding a touch of sweetness to their savoury dishes.

1 Heat 2 tablespoons of the olive oil in a frying pan. Add the onion and garlic and cook until softened and lightly golden.

2 Add the minced chicken, cinnamon, sugar, saffron, raisins and pistachios (if using), and fry lightly to infuse the meat with the aromatic spices. Cook for 8–10 minutes then transfer to a bowl and leave to cool.

3 Remove the filo pastry from the packet and keep it moist under a damp cloth. Cut each sheet into twenty squares of approximately 7cm.

4 Place a little of the cooled chicken mixture onto one corner of the filo pastry, then brush the edges with beaten egg. Fold the pastry over to make a triangle, pressing down to ensure the edges are firmly closed together. Brush liberally with beaten egg all over, then leave to rest for 30 minutes.

5 Heat the rest of the olive oil to 160°C/325°F in a pan, and cook the pastries for 2–3 minutes, until golden. Remove, and dust liberally with icing sugar.

4 tablespoons virgin olive oil

1 small aubergine *cut into 5mm cubes*

1 onion *finely chopped*

½ teaspoon ground cumin

sea salt and freshly ground black pepper

2 ripe firm tomatoes *cut into small cubes*

75g cooked spinach *chopped*

1 garlic clove *crushed*

½ teaspoon sumac

2 tablespoons pine nuts

350g shortcrust pastry

a little beaten egg

50g fresh mackerel fillets *boned and cut into 5cm lengths*

mackerel fatayer

Fatayer is the name of a small Lebanese pastry. In Lebanon, it is often stuffed with spinach, but almost any filling could be used. Minced lamb and feta go particularly well together, but here I use mackerel, which works beautifully, too. Try flavouring some yoghurt with mint or sumac as an accompaniment.

1 Preheat the oven to 200°C/400°F/gas mark 6.

2 Heat 3 tablespoons of the olive oil in a large frying pan, add the aubergine cubes and fry for 8–10 minutes until golden. Add the onion and cumin and cook for a further 2 minutes. Season to taste. Transfer the mixture to a bowl and leave to cool.

3 Heat the remaining oil in the pan and add the tomatoes, spinach, garlic, sumac and pine nuts. Cook until almost dry in texture. Season to taste.

4 Roll out the pastry to 3mm thick and cut out twelve 7.5cm rounds using a cookie cutter. Brush the edges with the beaten egg.

5 Place a heaped spoonful of the aubergine mixture in the centre of each round, then top with a spoonful of the spinach and tomato mixture. Finally, top with a section of seasoned mackerel. Roll up the pastry, seal, then gently twist and press each end using your your thumb and index finger.

6 Place the pies on a baking sheet and brush the exterior surfaces with more beaten egg. Bake for 15–20 minutes until golden.

pg tip Sumac is a lemon-tasting red berry that is dried and ground, and used extensively in salads, and to flavour meat and fish dishes, throughout Lebanon, Syria and Israel. It is available from Middle Eastern stores.

500g baby octopus *heads and beaks removed, cleaned*
4 tablespoons virgin olive oil

for the zhoug
½ small onion *chopped*
2 garlic cloves *crushed*
1 teaspoon sugar
small bunch of fresh coriander
½ teaspoon coriander seeds
½ teaspoon cumin seeds
3 green chillies *deseeded and chopped*
200ml virgin olive oil

chargrilled baby octopus with green zhoug

Baby octopus can be obtained from any good fishmonger, although there are also some good-quality frozen ones available. Failing that, you could use squid, cut into large pieces.

1 First, make the zhoug. Place the onion, garlic, sugar and fresh coriander into a small blender and blitz briefly.

2 In a dry frying pan, toast the coriander and cumin seeds, along with the chopped green chillies, for 1 minute. Add to the blender and blitz. With the motor running, gradually add the olive oil through the feeder tube to form a thick relish-style sauce.

3 Place the octopus in a dish, pour over the olive oil and the zhoug and mix well together. Cover and refrigerate for 2 hours.

4 To serve, remove the octopus from its marinade and place on a preheated hot grill. Cook, turning regularly and brushing regularly with the reserved zhoug marinade, for 6–8 minutes, or until cooked.

for the pork

400g pork fillet *cut into large cubes*

2 tablespoons virgin olive oil

2 tablespoons white wine vinegar

1 garlic clove *crushed*

1 teaspoon cumin seeds

1 teaspoon smoked paprika

for the muhammara

3 red peppers *roasted, peeled and deseeded*

¼ teaspoon red chilli flakes

75g ground walnuts

2 tablespoons *dibs rumen* (pomegranate molasses)

½ teaspoon ground cumin

2 tablespoons virgin olive oil (and a little extra for drizzling)

a little sugar

a little sea salt

½ tablespoon lemon juice

paprika, for dusting

cumin-spiced pork with muhammara

The odd-sounding *muhammara* is a traditional spice paste from the Yemen, not dissimilar to Tunisian harissa. If you like a little spice kick in your dip, look no further. The chilli adds real 'umph' to the *muhammara*, while the roasted peppers and molasses add a pleasingly smoky sweetness.

1 Marinate the pork cubes in the oil, vinegar, garlic, cumin seeds and paprika overnight.
2 For the muhammara, place the peppers, chilli flakes, walnuts, molasses and cumin in a blender and blitz to a smooth and creamy purée. Transfer to a bowl, beat in the olive oil, sugar and salt, and finish with lemon juice to taste.
3 Divide the pork onto four presoaked wooden or bamboo skewers, and cook on a preheated hot grill for 4–5 minutes until golden and cooked through.
4 Spoon the muhammara onto a serving dish, drizzle over a little olive oil and dust with paprika. Arrange the skewers on the bed of muhammara and serve.

pg tip Pomegranate molasses *(dibs rumen)* is a wonder syrup used widely in Middle Eastern cooking. It tastes fantastic added to meat stews, or when used to add a little sourness to braised dishes. It's well worth digging out a speciality store that sells it.

175g cracked wheat (burgul)

1 x 400g tin chickpeas *drained*

3 spring onions *finely chopped*

3 tablespoons chopped mint

2 tablespoons chopped flat-leaf parsley

juice of 2 lemons

100ml virgin olive oil

½ teaspoon ground cinnamon

sea salt and freshly ground black pepper

1 little gem lettuce, to serve

saffi

This Lebanese cracked wheat salad is one step up from the traditional tabbouleh. Try adding grilled prawns or some other seafood to the finished salad.

1 Place the cracked wheat in a large bowl and add enough cold water to cover. Set aside for 15 minutes, then drain well, squeezing the grains between your hands to extract all the excess water. Return to the bowl.

2 Add the chickpeas and remaining ingredients (except the lettuce), season to taste, and toss well.

3 Serve with the little gem lettuce, whose sturdy leaves can be used to scoop up the saffi for eating.

400g pork fillet *cut into 2.5cm cubes*

100ml virgin olive oil

1 small onion *finely chopped*

1 garlic clove *crushed*

1 tablespoon chopped mint (plus some for garnishing)

1 tablespoon paprika

½ tablespoon ground cumin

juice of 1 lemon

country bread, to serve

for the dip

125ml natural yoghurt

¼ teaspoon ground cinnamon

¼ teaspoon ground cumin

¼ teaspoon ground ginger

sea salt and freshly ground black pepper

moorish kebabs with a spicy dip

Kebabs were first introduced to Europe by Arabs from North Africa. They were made with lamb originally, but nowadays pork is often the preferred meat.

1 In a bowl, mix the meat with all the remaining ingredients, cover with clingfilm and marinate overnight, allowing time for you to turn the mixture occasionally.

2 When ready to serve, thread equal amounts of pork onto eight presoaked wooden or bamboo skewers. Place on a preheated grill pan and cook, turning regularly, until golden and cooked through.

3 Meanwhile, mix the dip ingredients together and season to taste.

4 Scatter the kebabs with the remaining mint and serve with the dip and large chunks of country bread.

4 tablespoons virgin olive oil

4 large boneless quails (available from good stores) *skinned*

25g unsalted butter (plus extra for brushing the pastry)

1 onion *finely chopped*

1 teaspoon ground cardamom

good pinch of saffron filaments

1 teaspoon ground cinnamon

50g ground walnuts

1 tablespoon chopped coriander

1 tablespoon chopped flat-leaf parsley

8 sheets filo pastry

for the salsa

1 tablespoon olive oil

1 tablespoon lemon juice

1 tablespoon runny honey

1 cooked beetroot *peeled and cut into 1cm dice*

1 orange *peeled, flesh cut into 1cm dice*

1 small red onion *peeled and cut into 1cm dice*

6 green pitted olives *cut into 1cm dice*

2 tablespoons freshly chopped coriander

quail baklava with beetroot, olive and orange salsa

You're right, baklava is a classic Middle Eastern sweet made from honey, nuts and filo pastry. In typical PG style, however, I have created my own savoury version, using young quails. I hope you agree that it tastes good.

1 Heat half of the olive oil in a non stick-frying pan. When hot, add the quails, fry quickly until golden, then remove.

2 Add the butter to the frying pan, along with the onion, cardamom, saffron, cinnamon and walnuts, and cook over a low heat. Return the quails to the pan, mix with the spices and herbs, then cover the pan with a lid and cook gently for 5–6 minutes. Remove from the heat and transfer to a bowl to cool.

3 To make the baklava, brush the filo sheets liberally with melted butter, placing one on top of another. When you have used up all the sheets, cut the layered pastry in half vertically and horizontally to form four squares.

4 Place one quail and some of the filling in the centre of each square, then bring the four edges up to seal the quail in the centre. Turn the baklava over and place it on a plate. Prepare the other three in the same way, then leave them to rest for 30 minutes in the fridge.

5 Meanwhile, make the salsa. Simply mix all the ingredients together in a bowl, then leave to marinate for 30 minutes.

6 When ready to serve, heat the remaining oil in a non-stick frying pan, add the baklavas, and cook over a medium heat for 3–4 minutes on each side, until golden and crispy.

225g boiled new potatoes *peeled*
125g feta cheese *crumbled*
2 tablespoons chopped mint
sea salt and freshly ground black pepper
6 sheets filo pastry
3 tablespoons virgin olive oil

potato, feta and mint tiropites

The beauty of these little pastries is that they freeze extremely well (uncooked), for up to one month. Replacing the potato with aubergine or peppers tastes equally good.

1 Preheat the oven to 220°C/425°F/gas mark 7.
2 Dry the hot peeled potatoes in a dry pan over a low heat. Roughly mash them, then remove from the pan and leave to cool.
3 Stir in the crumbled feta cheese and mint, and season to taste.
4 While assembling the tiropites, keep the filo pastry covered with a damp tea towel. Working on one sheet of filo pastry at a time, brush the pastry lightly with some olive oil then cut it into three long strips.
5 Place 1 tablespoon of filling at the top of one filo strip. Fold the corner of the filo over the filling, so that the top edge of the pastry is now over the right edge. Take the point of the strip and fold this down towards the bottom of the pastry. Continue to fold this way to make a pastry-filled triangle. Repeat with the other strips, followed by the other sheets.
6 Transfer the pastry parcels to baking trays and brush with the remaining oil.
7 Cook at the top of the oven for 18–20 minutes, until crisp and golden. Serve warm.

sardines with pickled chilli and olives

4 tablespoons virgin olive oil

8 medium-size fresh sardines *scaled, gutted and butterflied (head removed)*

coarse sea salt

4 garlic cloves *crushed*

a pinch of saffron filaments

1 tablespoon smoked paprika

2 bay leaves

12 black olives *pitted*

2 Lebanese pickled chillies (or 1 small red or green chilli, chopped) *shredded finely*

pinch of sugar

75ml white wine vinegar

My take on a Spanish *escabeche* uses Lebanese pickled chillies and saffron as the dominant flavourings. Any type of oily fish, including mullet or mackerel, works well.

1 First prepare the sardines for marinating. Starting from the head end, roll up each sardine tightly, and secure by piercing a cocktail stick through the tail.

2 Heat the olive oil in a non-stick frying pan, season the sardines with sea salt and fry them on both sides for 2–3 minutes. Transfer to a shallow dish.

3 Strain the oil used for cooking the sardines and clean the frying pan. Return the oil to the pan, add the garlic, saffron and paprika, and fry gently for 1 minute. Add the bay leaves, olives, chillies, sugar and wine vinegar, along with 100ml water. Simmer gently for 2 minutes.

4 Pour the liquid over the sardines and leave to marinate for 3–4 hours, to allow the flavours to infuse into the fish.

5 Serve at room temperature.

tunisian fishcakes

350g fresh mackerel fillet *skinned and cut into large pieces*

¼ teaspoon ground turmeric

½ teaspoon ground cumin

½ teaspoon ground coriander

2.5cm piece root ginger *peeled and finely grated*

1 teaspoon harissa

4 tablespoons virgin olive oil

300g cold mashed potatoes (nothing added)

sea salt and freshly ground black pepper

for the coating

a little flour

1 egg *beaten*

50g fresh white breadcrumbs

25g couscous

for the sauce

100ml mayonnaise

1 teaspoon harissa

1 teaspoon grated root ginger

The coating of the fishcakes in couscous gives an interesting texture to this dish.

1 Place the mackerel pieces in a shallow dish. Add the spices, ginger, harissa and half the olive oil. Mix well and lightly massage into the fish, then cover with clingfilm and refrigerate for 4 hours.

2 Mix the sauce ingredients in a small bowl and refrigerate until needed.

3 Remove the fish from the marinade and place in a medium-size non-stick frying pan. Add 100ml water, cover, and cook for 3–4 minutes over a low heat, until tender. Remove and dry off any excess liquid. Leave to cool a little, then flake into a bowl.

4 When the fish is cold, add the mashed potato and mix thoroughly together. Season to taste. Divide the mixture into eight equal portions and roll into balls.

5 Dip the balls in a little flour, then in the beaten egg, and finally in the mixed breadcrumbs and couscous. Flatten them slightly, then cook in the remaining olive oil in a non-stick pan, until golden and crispy. Drain on kitchen paper and serve with the sauce on the side.

200ml natural set yoghurt

3 spring onions *finely chopped*

2 small green chillies *deseeded and finely chopped*

1 tablespoon white wine vinegar

2 garlic cloves *crushed*

sea salt

1 fresh pomegranate *halved and seeds removed*

2 tablespoons freshly chopped dill

2 tablespoons freshly chopped mint

a little virgin olive oil

labna with green chilli and pomegranate

Labna, a lovely refreshing dip made from strained yoghurt, is extremely popular in the Middle East. This recipe has great flavour, lots of colour, and tastes good either chilled or at room temperature. It's a perfect dip for dunking Middle Eastern-style flatbreads into.

1 In a bowl, mix the yoghurt with the spring onions, chillies, vinegar and garlic. Season with salt.

2 Transfer to a serving bowl and sprinkle with the pomegranate seeds, dill and mint. Drizzle over the olive oil and serve with Middle Eastern-style flatbread, such as pitta or *lavosh*.

pg tip Middle Eastern flatbreads are very easy to make at home, but they are also widely available to buy, too. *Khubz* and *lavosh* make a nice change from the ubiquitous pitta, and can also serve as a wrap for all manner of fillings.

400g chicken thighs *skinned and boned*

8 bay leaves

8 large pitted green olives

2 tablespoons virgin olive oil

30g preserved lemons *pith removed and finely chopped*

2 tablespoons freshly chopped coriander

for the marinade

1 garlic clove *crushed*

3 tablespoons virgin olive oil

½ teaspoon ground cardamom

¼ teaspoon ground cinnamon

2.5cm piece root ginger *peeled and grated*

persian chicken brochettes

Preserved (or salted) lemons, which are used extensively in North African cooking, are available in good delis. They add an unmistakable, salty citric taste to these marinated chicken skewers.

1 Mix the ingredients for the marinade together in a bowl, add the chicken thighs, cover, and refrigerate overnight. The next day, cut the chicken into bite-size pieces.

2 When ready to serve, brush a ridged grill pan with a little olive oil and put it on the heat. Place the chicken pieces on the hot pan and cook for about 5 minutes, until tender. Remove from the heat and keep warm.

3 While the pan is still hot, grill the bay leaves and the olives, the latter only lightly. Once all three ingredients are grilled, thread one of each onto eight wooden skewers: one chicken piece, one bay leaf and one olive, in that order.

4 Transfer to a serving dish, mix the preserved lemons and coriander together and sprinkle over the brochettes to serve.

the spice route

Along the Spice Route, in India, Thailand, Malaysia and Indonesia, bite-size foods are imbued with the tantalising flavours and aromas of ginger, coriander, lemongrass, turmeric and chilli.

Indian spices in bowls

300g raw king prawns *shelled and deveined*

½ teaspoon grated root ginger

⅛ teaspoon each: chilli powder, turmeric and chaat masala

½ teaspoon mild curry powder

1 egg white

1 tablespoon chickpea flour (gram flour)

sea salt and freshly ground black pepper

4 slices thick white sliced bread *crusts removed*

vegetable oil, for frying

for the sambal

2 ripe plum tomatoes *chopped*

½ red onion *chopped*

2 tablespoons chopped coriander

juice of 2 limes

1 teaspoon cumin seeds *toasted and crushed*

curried prawn toasts with tomato sambal

A play on the traditional prawn toasts seen endlessly on Chinese menus, these have a more spicy Indian feel.

1 For the sambal, mix all the ingredients in a bowl, then set aside for 1 hour for the flavours to infuse.

2 Place the prawns, ginger, spices and egg white in the food processor and blitz to a paste. Transfer to a bowl, fold in the chickpea flour and season to taste.

3 Spread the prawn mixture onto the slices of bread, ensuring an even coating.

4 Heat the oil to 160°C/325°F in a frying pan. Fry the bread with the prawn mixture face down for just 20 seconds, until golden and crisp, then flip the bread over to brown the other side. Drain on kitchen paper.

5 Cut the toasts into quarters and serve with the sambal.

1 large baking potato (approx 350g)

100g tinned sweetcorn *well drained*

1 tablespoon chickpea flour (gram flour)

3 tablespoons vegetable oil

2 green chillies *deseeded and finely chopped*

2 spring onions *finely chopped*

½ teaspoon ground cumin

½ teaspoon ground coriander

2 tablespoons freshly chopped coriander

sea salt and freshly ground black pepper

aloo corn tikki

One of India's culinary glories is its comforting street food, sold on every street corner. These potato patties are one such street delicacy. Tamarind chutney makes a good accompaniment.

1 Preheat the oven to 180°C/350°F/gas mark 4.

2 Place the potato on a baking tray in the oven and bake for 1 hour and 15 minutes. When cooked, remove and leave to cool.

3 Peel the potato, then place in a bowl and crush lightly. Add the sweetcorn and chickpea flour.

4 Heat 1 tablespoon of the oil in a small frying pan, add the chillies, spring onions and spices, and cook for 30 seconds. Add this to the potato and mix well. Add the chopped coriander and season with salt and pepper.

5 Divide the potato mixture into equal-size balls, then shape into small patties. Heat the remaining oil in a frying pan, add the patties, and fry until golden and crisp.

1 teaspoon ground cumin

1 teaspoon coriander seeds *crushed*

½ teaspoon garlic salt

1 tablespoon paprika

1 teaspoon red chilli flakes

1 teaspoon ground ginger

2 teaspoons sea salt

4 x 120g salmon fillets *skinned and boned*

vegetable oil

lime slices, to garnish

bengali blackened salmon

The process of 'blackening' food – quick searing in spices to produce a blackened crust – is traditionally a preparation used in Cajun cooking. Here's my fusion-style variation from farther east. The salmon looks great served on a banana leaf, and tastes good with mint- or tamarind-flavoured yoghurt.

1 Mix together all the spices and the salt, then use to rub into both sides of the salmon pieces. Place the fish on a tray, cover, and leave at room temperature for 30 minutes.

2 When ready to serve, heat up a frying pan over a high heat. Add a little oil to the pan, then cook the fillets for 2 minutes without moving them. Turn the fish over, cover, and cook for a further 2 minutes. While the exterior should look blackened, the fish should be lightly cooked inside.

3 Serve garnished with some thin slices of lime.

275g firm white fish fillet (e.g. sole, haddock or halibut) *boned and skinned*

50g chickpea flour (gram flour)

1 red onion *finely chopped*

2 spring onions *finely chopped*

2 green chillies *deseeded and finely chopped*

1 tablespoon chopped coriander

1 teaspoon ground cumin

pinch of bicarbonate of soda

sea salt and freshly ground black pepper

vegetable oil, for deep-frying

fish pakoras

Pakoras are simple Indian fritters that are made by binding pieces of fish, meat or vegetable in a batter made of chickpea flour, then frying them until crisp.

1 Chop the fish coarsely and place in a bowl. Stir in the flour and just enough water to make a thick batter coating around the fish. Add the remaining ingredients, excluding the oil.

2 Heat the oil to 160°C/325°F in a frying pan. Using a spoon, drop equal amounts of the batter into the hot oil, in batches, and cook for 3–4 minutes or until the pakoras are cooked and crispy golden. Drain on kitchen paper.

1 large red chilli *finely chopped*

2 garlic cloves *crushed*

75g cashew nuts *chopped*

1 tablespoon sesame oil

2 tablespoons chopped coriander leaves

2 tablespoons tomato ketchup

½ teaspoon sugar

475g swordfish fillet *boneless*

juice of 2 limes

sea salt

2 sheets banana leaf

a little oil, for greasing

spicy sambal fish in banana leaf

You could replace the swordfish with tuna in this recipe if you wish. Either way, serve the fish still in its banana leaf for an eye-catching presentation.

1 Place the chilli, garlic, nuts and sesame oil in a mortar, or small blender, and grind or blitz to a coarse pulp. Transfer the mixture to a bowl, add the coriander, ketchup and sugar, and mix well.

2 Cut the swordfish into four equal-size pieces and place in a dish. Squeeze over the lime juice, season with salt, then cover and leave to marinate at room temperature for 30 minutes.

3 Remove the swordfish from the marinade, dry it well, then rub the spice paste onto both sides of the fish.

4 Soften the banana leaves by dipping them in very hot water until they become pliant. This takes about 30 seconds. Dry the leaves, then grease with a little oil. Place a piece of fish in the centre of each leaf, then fold the edges up to form a moneybag shape, securing the top with raffia, kitchen string, a cocktail stick or even a skewer.

5 Steam the fish parcels over simmering water, covered, for 8–10 minutes or until cooked through.

2 tablespoons vegetable oil

1 small onion *finely chopped*

¼ teaspoon ground turmeric

1 tablespoon curry powder

¼ teaspoon chilli powder

225g minced lamb

sea salt and freshly ground pepper

1 tablespoon chopped mint

40g mature Cheddar cheese

1 egg *beaten*

4 naan breads

filled indian naans

These naan breads, filled with a spicy, cheesy lamb mixture, are satisfying to make and even more satisfying to unwrap when cooked.

1 Preheat the oven to 180°C/350°F/gas mark 4.

2 Heat the oil in a large frying pan. When hot, add the onion, ground spices, and cook for 2–3 minutes to infuse the flavours.

3 Add the minced lamb and fry until the meat is sealed all over, cooked through, and almost dry in texture. Remove from the heat and leave to cool.

4 Season the cooled lamb to taste, add the mint and cheese, then bind with the egg. Spread this mixture onto two of the naan breads, then top each one with a second naan, pressing down well to compact the filling.

5 Wrap each stuffed naan in foil, ensuring that they are fairly tightly wrapped. Place on a baking sheet in the oven for 10–12 minutes.

6 Allow the filled naan to cool slightly before serving, cut into strips.

350g mashed potato

2 tablespoons chopped coriander leaves

1 tablespoon chopped mint leaves

1 red chilli *deseeded and finely chopped*

1 garlic clove *crushed*

100g paneer cheese *coarsely grated*

sea salt and freshly ground black pepper

juice of ½ lemon

60g chickpea flour (gram flour)

pinch of baking powder

pinch of chilli powder

vegetable oil, for deep-frying

potato bonda

This classic Indian potato dish is easy to prepare and extremely good to eat. You should be able to find paneer cheese, an Indian curd cheese, in your local Indian shop.

1 In a bowl, mix the mashed potato with the herbs, chilli, garlic and grated paneer cheese. Add the lemon juice and season with salt and pepper. Shape the mixture into walnut-size balls in the palm of your hands.

2 Mix the chickpea flour and baking powder together in a bowl, and season with salt and chilli powder. Add sufficient water to form a thickish batter.

3 Heat the vegetable oil in a frying pan to 160°C/325°F.

4 Dip the potato balls in the batter, ensuring that they are completely coated, then drop them into the hot oil. Fry for 1–2 minutes, until golden.

5 Drain on kitchen paper.

pg tip A dip of mint-flavoured yoghurt sweetened with a touch of honey makes a great accompaniment to this dish.

250g minced beef

150g minced lamb

1 small onion *finely chopped*

1 garlic clove *crushed*

½ teaspoon ground ginger

½ teaspoon ground cumin

1 teaspoon ground cardamom

50g stoneless dates *chopped*

2 tablespoons chopped mint

sea salt and freshly ground black pepper

2 eggs

3 teaspoons rose-water

2 tablespoons vegetable oil

meatballs with dates and rose-water

Rose-water is used extensively in Southern Asian cuisine, primarily in sweet dishes. It has a very distinct flavour and perfume, and gives a distinctly exotic touch to these meatballs.

1 In a large bowl, mix together the two meats, onion, garlic, spices, dates and mint. Season with salt and pepper.

2 Work the meat together, add the eggs, and work again until thoroughly mixed. Add the rose-water and leave to infuse for 30 minutes at room temperature.

3 Using wet hands, shape the mixture into small meatballs, then lightly flatten them.

4 Heat the oil in a frying pan, then fry the meatballs for 3–4 minutes, turning them once.

1 garlic clove *crushed*
1 red chilli *finely chopped*
2cm piece root ginger *peeled and grated*
1 shallot *finely sliced*
600g medium-size clams
juice of 1 lime
2 tablespoons *nam pla* (Thai fish sauce)
20g unsalted butter *chilled and cut into small pieces*
2 tablespoons roughly chopped coriander

thai-style clams

Clams are delicious but sometimes difficult to get hold of, in which case you could use mussels instead.

1 Place the garlic, chilli, ginger and shallot in a wide-based pan and place the clams on top. Add 150ml water, cover with a tight-fitting lid, and bring rapidly to the boil.
2 Cook for 2 minutes, shaking the pan regularly, until the clams open. Discard any clams that do not open.
3 Add the lime juice, fish sauce and butter, and stir to combine. Transfer to a serving dish, including all the pan juices, and scatter over the coriander.

1 tablespoon vegetable oil
½ onion *finely chopped*
2.5cm piece root ginger *peeled and grated*
75g cooked potatoes *peeled and cut into small dice*
pinch of turmeric
¼ teaspoon chilli powder
2 teaspoons mild curry powder
300g chicken breast *boned and skinned*
sea salt and freshly ground black pepper
pinch of sugar
350g shortcrust pastry

chicken puffs

These puffs originated quite by accident, when I was asked by an Asian guest for a canapé made with spicy chicken. They remain a feature on my cocktail menu.

1 Heat the oil in a non-stick frying pan. Add the onion and ginger and fry until the onion turns light golden brown. Add the potatoes, turmeric, chilli powder and curry powder, and cook for a further minute.
2 Cut the chicken into small dice and add to the pan, along with 4 tablespoons of water. Cover with a lid and cook for 6–8 minutes, until the chicken is cooked and the mixture almost dry. Add some salt and pepper and a little sugar. Remove from the heat and leave to cool.
3 Roll out the pastry to 3mm thick, then cut out circles using a 7.5cm cookie cutter.
4 Spoon some of the chicken filling into the centre of each pastry round, then fold the pastry over to form a crescent. Crimp the edges to seal. Place in the fridge to rest for 30 minutes.
5 These pastries can either be baked, for 20–25 minutes at 160°C/325°F/gas mark 3, or deep-fried until golden and crisp. Serve warm.

100g fresh white breadcrumbs

3 tablespoons freshly chopped coriander

50g unsweetened coconut flakes

8 stalks fresh lemongrass

425g white fish fillets (e.g. cod or halibut) *boned and skinned*

1 small red chilli *deseeded and finely chopped*

2 tablespoons light soy sauce

2 spring onions *finely chopped*

3 eggs

2 teaspoons cornflour

zest of 1 lime

a little flour for dipping

4 tablespoons vegetable oil, for frying

for the mayonnaise

3 tablespoons mayonnaise

splash of lime juice *to taste*

dash of chilli oil

5mm piece root ginger *peeled and grated*

lemongrass fishcake skewers with lime-spiked mayonnaise

In this recipe, the lemongrass acts not only as a skewer, but also adds flavour. All you need to complement the fishcakes is the Asian-inspired mayonnaise and a nice crisp salad.

1 In a bowl, mix together the breadcrumbs, coriander and coconut flakes, and set aside.

2 Clean the lemongrass and remove the tough outer casing. Finely chop two of the stalks, leaving the other four intact.

3 Cut the fish pieces into large chunks and put them in a blender. Add the chopped lemongrass, chilli, soy sauce, spring onions and two of the eggs. Blitz the mixture for 20–30 seconds, until you have a smooth paste.

4 Spoon the fish mixture into a bowl, stir in the cornflour and lime zest, then divide into twelve evenly sized balls. Shape the balls into round, flat patties, then dip them in turn in a little flour, the remaining egg (beaten), and finally into the coconut, coriander and breadcrumb mixture.

5 Carefully thread two fishcakes onto each remaining lemongrass stalk; you may need to mould them on to make sure they are secure. Heat the oil in a large frying pan, then add the fish skewers and cook for 2 minutes on each side, until golden and crispy.

6 Drain the fishcakes on kitchen paper then serve with the mayonnaise, made by simply mixing all the ingredients together.

400g firm white fish fillets (e.g. monkfish, sole or halibut)

vegetable oil, for deep-frying

4 kaffir lime leaves *shredded*

3 spring onions *thinly shredded*

for the sauce

2 tablespoons red curry paste

125ml coconut milk

1 teaspoon *nam pla* (Thai fish sauce)

1 teaspoon caster sugar

1 teaspoon dried shrimp paste

crispy fish in red curry

In Thailand they prepare this dish using a local fish, called *pla chron*, which is similar to mackerel. Personally, I prefer to use a firm-textured white fish.

1 First make the sauce. Mix the curry paste with the coconut milk, place in a pan, and cook gently for 4–5 minutes, until the sauce thickens.

2 Add the fish sauce, sugar and shrimp paste. Heat through, then set aside.

3 Cut the fish into bite-size pieces and fry in hot oil until crisp and golden. Drain on kitchen paper.

4 Place the crispy fish in a dish, pour over the curry sauce, and garnish with the shredded lime leaves and onions.

sweet chicken in pandanus jackets

2 shallots *peeled*
4 garlic cloves *peeled*
2.5cm piece root ginger *peeled and grated*
2 green chillies *deseeded*
1 teaspoon Chinese five-spice powder
2 tablespoons hoisin sauce
1 tablespoon sesame oil
400g chicken thighs *skinned and boned*
8 pandanus leaves *washed and dried*
vegetable oil, for deep-frying

Pandanus leaves grow profusely in Thailand (where they are known as *pandan*) and are available from good florists in Britain. When used as a wrapper for chicken or fish, they impart a wonderfully earthy and exotic flavour during cooking.

1 Using a pestle and mortar, grind the shallots, garlic, ginger and chillies to a coarse paste. Add the five-spice powder, hoisin and sesame oil, and mix well.
2 Transfer to a bowl, add the chicken thighs, and rub the paste thoroughly into the meat. Leave to marinate for 4 hours.
3 Wrap each chicken thigh in a pandanus leaf, as though you were wrapping a parcel, and use a cocktail stick to secure it.
4 Heat the vegetable oil to 160°C/325°F. Immerse the leaves into the hot oil and cook for 5–6 minutes.
5 Serve each pandanus parcel on an individual plate, allowing each diner to unwrap their own leaves.

lambchops in green masala

8 small lambchops
2 green chillies
2 garlic cloves *crushed*
2cm piece root ginger *peeled and grated*
handful of coriander *leaves only*
1 teaspoon natural yoghurt
juice of 1 lemon
sea salt

The green masala curry paste used in this recipe is a great base for chicken and lamb dishes. Desiccated coconut can be added to the paste, and the result is equally delicious.

1 Trim the chops free of all fat and clean the bones thoroughly.
2 Place the chillies, garlic, ginger and coriander in a blender, along with the yoghurt and one quarter of the lemon juice, and blitz to a smooth paste.
3 Rub the paste over the chops, place them in a dish, cover with clingfilm, and refrigerate overnight.
4 When ready to serve, heat a grill pan until almost smoking. Sprinkle the chops with salt and cook on the grill for 2–3 minutes, or until charred all over.
5 Arrange the chops on serving dishes, squeeze over the remaining lemon juice, and serve.

grilled scallops with coriander and lime pickle

12 fresh scallops *cleaned, on the half shell*
sea salt and freshly ground black pepper
1 tablespoon mild curry powder
25g unsalted butter

for the pickle
2 tablespoons virgin olive oil
1 onion *finely chopped*
2 garlic cloves *crushed*
1 small green chilli *deseeded and finely chopped*
2.5cm piece root ginger *peeled and finely grated*
2 tablespoons *nam pla* (Thai fish sauce)
zest and juice of 4 limes (plus extra lime wedges to garnish)
sea salt and freshly ground black pepper
2 tablespoons freshly chopped coriander

Grilling scallops brings out their natural sweetness to great effect, and the spicy lime pickle acts as the perfect foil. This recipe is a big favourite with my family.

1 First, make the pickle. Heat the olive oil in a pan, add the onion, garlic, chilli and ginger, and cook over a low heat until softened.
2 Add the fish sauce and lime zest and juice, along with a little seasoning. Cook over a low heat, until the mixture is very soft and aromatic. This will take about 15 minutes. Add the coriander and cook for a further 5 minutes. Transfer to a bowl and leave to cool.
3 Preheat the grill to its highest setting.
4 Season each scallop liberally with salt, then sprinkle on a little pepper and dust with curry powder.
5 Place a good spoonful of pickle in the bottom of each of the scallop shells. Top with a scallop, followed by a knob of butter. Place on a large grill sheet.
6 When the grill is hot, pop the scallops under for 2–3, minutes or until just cooked. (Do not overcook the scallops as they will become tough.) Transfer the scallops to a dish and garnish with the lime wedges.

chilli prawns with curry leaf and coconut

12 large raw prawns *peeled, leaving the head and tail intact*
1 tablespoon vegetable oil
1 garlic glove *crushed*
10 curry leaves
10g unsalted butter
pinch of sea salt
1 large red chilli *chopped*
125g unsweetened desiccated coconut
1 teaspoon soy sauce
1 teaspoon red wine vinegar

Curry leaves have a pronounced flavour that goes fantastically with coconut and chilli.

1 First, you need to devein the prawns (see tip). Then wash and dry them, and place in a bowl. Add the oil, garlic and curry leaves, and set aside for 20–30 minutes.
2 Heat a wok until almost smoking. Throw in the prawns in their marinade and toss them, adding the sea salt and butter.
3 Add the remaining ingredients and stir-fry briskly for 2–3 minutes. Remove from the heat and serve immediately.

pg tip The black 'vein' running down the back of the prawn is the intestinal tract. It is not harmful if eaten, but the prawn looks better without it. Using a small, sharp knife, simply make a shallow incision along the back of the prawn, then carefully remove any black vein with the tip of the knife.

15g freshly chopped mint
1 red chilli *deseeded and finely diced*
½ teaspoon chaat masala
¼ teaspoon chilli powder
¼ teaspoon turmeric
zest and juice of 1 lemon
1 tablespoon brown sugar
2 tablespoons natural yoghurt
175g paneer cheese *cut into 8 large batons*
4 large red peppers
2 tablespoons virgin olive oil

spicy paneer-baked peppers with lemon and chilli

I love the versatility of paneer cheese. I often use it in curries, or grill it (after marinating) in tandoori or tikka spices. It's also great wrapped in pitta bread as part of a veggie sandwich. Basically, paneer is an all-round excellent cheese that doesn't melt or lose its shape when heated.

1 In a bowl, mix together the mint, chilli, chaat masala, chilli powder, turmeric, lemon juice and zest, brown sugar and yoghurt. Add the cheese, cover with clingfilm, and leave to marinate overnight in the fridge.

2 The following day, preheat the oven to 200°C/400°F/gas mark 6.

3 Lay out a large sheet of foil on a work surface, place the peppers in the centre, and drizzle over a little olive oil. Scrunch up the foil to secure the peppers within, place on a baking tray, and roast in the oven for about 25 minutes. They should be soft but not overcooked. Remove and leave to cool.

4 Cut the cold peppers in half vertically, and clean out the inner seeds. Place a baton of marinated cheese in each pepper and roll it to secure the cheese inside. Secure with a cocktail stick, then lightly flatten with the palm of your hand.

5 Place the rolled peppers on the baking tray, drizzle over the remaining oil and bake in the oven for 10 minutes, or until the pepper begins to char and the cheese softens.

6 Remove the cocktail sticks before serving.

pg tip Chaat masala, available ready-made in Asian grocery stores, is a spice mix consisting of dried mango powder, cumin, black salt, coriander, dried ginger and red pepper. Normally added to dishes at the end of cooking, it offers a pungent smell and a sweet-sour flavour.

1 medium onion *chopped*
2.5cm piece root ginger *peeled and grated*
2 garlic cloves *crushed*
2 red chillies *finely chopped*
6 tablespoons virgin olive oil
1 tablespoon mild curry powder
½ teaspoon garam masala
150ml coconut milk
2 large raw prawns *peeled and deveined*
12 small pitted black olives
2 tablespoons freshly chopped coriander

stir-fried prawns with olives and coriander

The addition of olives to a spicy dish may seem unusual, but their saltiness really accentuates the flavours in the dish. It is fun to eat this dish using fingers of naan or paratha bread to wrap the prawns in.

1 Place half of the onion, the ginger, garlic and chillies in a small blender or food processor, and blitz to a paste.

2 Heat half the olive oil in a large frying pan or wok. Add the paste and stir-fry over a medium heat, until the paste browns slightly and becomes aromatic.

3 Mix the curry powder and garam masala with 2 tablespoons of water, add to the pan, and cook for 3–4 minutes. Add the coconut milk and simmer for a further 5 minutes.

4 Heat the remaining oil in another frying pan or wok. Add the remaining onion and fry for 3–4 minutes. Throw in the prawns and cook for 2 minutes, or until they turn red in colour.

5 Pour over the spicy sauce, add the olives and coriander, and mix well together. Transfer to a dish and serve piping hot.

1 tablespoon tikka paste

1 tablespoon natural yoghurt

½ teaspoon ground cumin

½ teaspoon ground cardamom

1 tablespoon chopped coriander

2cm piece root ginger *peeled and grated*

1 garlic clove *crushed*

400g minced chicken breast

a little oil

4 small naan breads

for the mint chutney

1 small bunch fresh mint

2cm piece root ginger *peeled and grated*

1 small green chilli *chopped*

juice of ½ lime

½ teaspoon sugar

1 teaspoon ground coriander

1 small onion, peeled and finely chopped

a little natural yoghurt, to blend (water is fine too)

sea salt and freshly ground black pepper

mini chicken tikka burgers with mint chutney

Burgers never lose their popularity, and these mini ones are always a talking point when I serve them. The mint chutney adds a nice Asian touch to the dish.

1 Place all the ingredients for the burgers (excluding the oil and naan breads) in a bowl and mix well. With wet hands, mould the mixture into twelve small burgers. Place these on a plate and refrigerate for 1 hour.

2 Meanwhile, make the chutney by placing all the ingredients in a blender with enough yoghurt or water to blitz to a thick sauce consistency. Season to taste.

3 Preheat a grill pan, then cook the burgers (brushed with a little oil) for 3–4 minutes on each side, until cooked through.

4 Meanwhile, cut each naan bread into three wedges, and toast until crispy. Top each naan wedge with a cooked burger and spear with a skewer.

鱿鱼 Deep Fried

Pan Fried So

豆 Braised

County Sty

辣毛 Fried

鸭 Fried Bu

水

Cuny Fried

景頤

Fried

the far east

In dim sum and sushi, China and Japan offer mystical little parcels of deliciousness that are perfect to share. They are packed with aromatic and flavourful combinations to tantalise your tastebuds and leave you wanting more.

2 tablespoons white miso

1 tablespoon dark brown sugar

2 tablespoons sake

1 tablespoon mirin

1 egg yolk

475g monkfish fillet *cleaned and cut into 2cm cubes*

1 teaspoon black sesame seeds

1 tablespoon vegetable oil

miso-glazed monkfish skewers

Miso, made by fermenting a mixture of soya beans, rice and cereal grains, is a thick paste used in Japan to flavour soups and sauces, season grilled foods, or to pickle vegetables, meat and fish. The two main types are red (strong and salty) and white (sweeter and milder in flavour), and these are the most widely available in this country.

1 Mix the miso, brown sugar, sake and mirin in a pan, then slowly bring to the boil. Reduce the heat and cook for 2–3 minutes, stirring occasionally. Add the egg yolk, then transfer to a shallow dish and cool.

2 Add the monkfish cubes, mix well with the marinade, then cover with clingfilm and refrigerate overnight.

3 When ready to serve, thread the monkfish cubes onto small metal or presoaked wooden skewers, and sprinkle with black sesame seeds.

4 Brush a ridged grill pan with oil and place on the heat. When very hot, place the skewers in the pan and cook for 5–6 minutes, turning them regularly and basting them with the marinade. Serve hot from the grill.

oriental oyster shooters

200ml tomato juice
4 tablespoons vodka
1 teaspoon wasabi paste
1 teaspoon mirin
½ teaspoon soy sauce
juice of 2 limes
1 teaspoon caster sugar
sea salt and freshly ground black pepper
8 very fresh oysters *shucked and cleaned*
1 lime, to garnish

I can never get enough of these little shooters. Created from a classic bloody mary shooter, they are packed with Asian flavour and, for me, are better than the original.

1 In a bowl, mix together all the ingredients except the oysters and lime, and season to taste. Refrigerate for 1 hour for the flavours to meld together.
2 To serve, place 2 oysters in the base of four small shot glasses, then pour over the shooter mix.
3 Garnish the glasses with lime wedges and serve chilled, with some chopsticks for digging out the oysters.

yakitori duck

3 tablespoons sake
4 tablespoons mirin
2 tablespoons caster sugar
4 tablespoons dark soy sauce
2 large duck breasts *skinned and boned*
150g small shiitake mushrooms *stalks removed*
2 tablespoons vegetable oil

Traditionally, *yakitori* (Japanese-style skewers) are made with chicken, but duck, and even pork and beef, are also superb cooked in this way. The sauce used to coat the chicken is traditionally used over and over again so that the flavour is rich and full. The skewers taste best when barbecued, but you can also cook them on a grill pan or under a grill.

1 Place the sake, mirin, sugar and soy sauce in a pan, bring to the boil, and simmer until reduced in volume by a third.
2 Cut the duck breasts in half, lengthways, then into large cubes, and place in a bowl. Pour over the marinade, add the mushrooms, cover with clingfilm and leave to marinate for 1 hour.
3 Drain the meat and the mushrooms, then thread them alternately onto presoaked wooden or bamboo skewers.
4 Cook on a preheated grill, brushed with a little oil, and cook until the skewered duck is beautifully charred and glossy, about 4–5 minutes.

pg tip Rice wine is an essential ingredient in Japanese and Chinese cookery, and is particularly useful in marinades and glazes. Chinese Shaoxing wine is often confused with Japanese sake, but the latter is more delicate in taste. Mirin, also from Japan, is essentially a sweetened sake. All three are widely available, but you can use dry sherry as a substitute, with the addition of a little extra sugar if you are using in place of mirin.

¼ cucumber

1 bunch watercress

100g cooked egg noodles

4 spring onions *finely sliced*

½ small cooked Chinese BBQ duck
(available from Asian stores)

for the dressing

2 stalks lemongrass *very finely chopped*

1 tablespoon rice wine vinegar

3 tablespoons peanut or vegetable oil

1 small red chilli *finely chopped*

2.5cm piece root ginger *peeled and grated*

chinese duck salad

It's amazing how such a tasty salad can be obtained from so few ingredients. Make sure you don't add the dressing until just before serving.

1 For the dressing, simply combine all the ingredients together in a bowl.

2 Cut the cucumber in half lengthways, scoop out the seeds with a teaspoon, then slice into half moons. Combine with the watercress, noodles and spring onions in a large bowl.

3 Remove the skin from the Chinese duck and cut into thin shreds. Add to the bowl.

4 Pour the dressing over the salad and toss gently together. Divide into bowls and serve.

hot spare ribs

600g American-style pork spare ribs
2 large garlic cloves *crushed*
½ teaspoon ground cumin
1 teaspoon chilli powder
1 teaspoon sesame oil
2 tablespoons vegetable oil
275ml chicken stock (or water)
1 tablespoon maple syrup
2 tablespoons dark soy sauce
4 tablespoons *char siu* (Chinese BBQ sauce)

Spare ribs, the most expensive cut of pork (from the lower portion of the belly and breastbone), are used in a variety of cuisines, including of course Chinese. They are best eaten by hand, so diners can simply gnaw the meat off the bone.

1 Cut the spare ribs into 5–7.5cm lengths, then cut between each rib to separate them. Place in a shallow dish.
2 Mix the garlic, cumin and chilli powder together in a bowl, then rub liberally into the flesh of the ribs. Cover and refrigerate overnight.
3 The next day, preheat the oven to 160°C/325°F/gas mark 3.
4 Heat both oils in a wok or large frying pan over a high heat, add the ribs, and fry until nicely browned all over. Add the remaining ingredients, then bring to the boil.
5 Transfer the spare ribs and the sauce to a large baking tray, ensuring that the ribs are in a single layer. Bake in the oven for 40–45 minutes, or until the ribs are cooked and dark in colour, and the sauce all but evaporated. Allow to cool slightly before serving.

pg tip *Char siu* is available in Asian stores, but you can make a reasonable approximation of it by simply mixing runny honey and dark soy sauce with a small amount of ground ginger and garlic.

japanese-style ceviche

425g very fresh salmon fillet *cleaned and skinned*
2.5cm piece root ginger *peeled and finely grated*
1 garlic clove *crushed*
1 teaspoon caster sugar
⅛ teaspoon wasabi paste
½ teaspoon sea salt
2 tablespoons shoyu (Japanese soy sauce)
100ml sake
1 tablespoons pickled ginger *finely chopped*
2 spring onions *finely chopped*
½ teaspoon black sesame seeds (optional)

Japanese cuisine is, in my opinion, one of the finest in the world. Food is prepared fresh and pure, particularly where fish is concerned. In an effort to conform, make sure that your salmon is as fresh as possible.

1 Cut the salmon, across the fillet, into 3mm-thick slices. Arrange in a single layer in the base of a shallow dish.
2 Place the grated ginger, garlic, sugar, wasabi and sea salt in a mortar and crush to a paste. Add the Japanese soy sauce, sake and pickled ginger, and stir well.
3 Pour the marinade over the salmon, cover with clingfilm, and refrigerate for 1 hour prior to serving.
4 When ready to serve, transfer the salmon to a serving plate, pour over the marinade, and sprinkle with the spring onions and black sesame seeds, if using.

200ml chicken stock
200ml coconut milk
2 tablespoons virgin olive oil
½ onion *finely chopped*
1 small garlic clove *crushed*
100g risotto rice (Arborio or Vialone Nano)
2 tablespoons chopped coriander
100g shiitake mushrooms *chopped*
2 spring onions *chopped*
2 eggs *beaten*
25g panko (Japanese breadcrumbs)
25g unsweetened desiccated coconut
vegetable oil, for frying

coconut shiitake risotto balls

The idea for this recipe arose out of Italy's famous rice balls (*supplì*), but I've played around with the flavours. So the rice is cooked in coconut milk and the balls are filled with shiitake mushrooms.

1 Combine the stock and coconut milk in a pan and bring to the boil. Maintain at a gentle simmer.

2 Heat half the olive oil in a thick-bottomed pan. Add the onion and garlic, and cook until the onion is softened. Add the rice and stir well.

3 Stir in the simmering stock a little at a time, and wait until the liquid has been absorbed before adding more, in the manner of a classic risotto. Cook until the rice is just tender and all the stock has been used and absorbed. The total cooking time will be 20–25 minutes. Stir in the coriander, then leave the risotto to cool.

4 Heat the remaining oil in a frying pan. When hot, add the mushrooms and the spring onions, and cook over a high heat for 2–3 minutes, until tender. Remove from the heat and leave to cool.

5 Divide the cold risotto into small, walnut-size balls, press some cooked mushroom and spring onion into the centre of each one, and roll to enclose.

6 Coat the risotto balls in beaten egg, then roll in a mixture of panko and desiccated coconut.

7 Fry in oil heated to 150°C/300°F, until golden, then drain on kitchen paper.

pg tip These risotto balls can be made in advance and frozen (unfried) for up to one month.

200g minced pork
2.5cm piece root ginger *peeled and grated*
2 garlic cloves *crushed*
sea salt and freshly ground black pepper
4 water chestnuts (tinned is fine) *chopped*
3 teaspoons freshly chopped coriander
100g cooked rice (preferably basmati or jasmine)
1 tablespoon *nam pla* **(Thai fish sauce)**
1 Chinese white cabbage *separated into leaves*

shanghai-style dolmades

Dolmades are a simple Greek dish of vine leaf rolls filled with savoury rice. They always remind me of a dish I had in the Far East, and here is my adaptation of that recipe. The stuffed leaves taste delicious dipped into either a sweet chilli sauce or a plum sauce spiked with Tabasco.

1 Mix the pork with the grated ginger and garlic, along with a liberal seasoning of salt and pepper. Add the chopped water chestnuts, coriander and rice, and season with the fish sauce.

2 Blanch the white cabbage leaves in boiling, salted water for 2–3 minutes, then refresh in iced water. Remove and dry in a cloth.

3 Cut away 5cm from the base of each cabbage leaf. Lay out eight of the larger leaves on a work surface, veined side down. Place an equal amount of pork mixture on the base of each leaf, then roll it up, tucking in the sides halfway to completely secure the filling.

4 Steam the rolls in a bamboo-style steamer over boiling water for 45 minutes, or until the pork is cooked through. Transfer the dolmades to a serving dish and serve.

pg tip If you can't get hold of Chinese white cabbage, you could use large bok choy leaves, blanched spinach leaves, or even normal white cabbage leaves (cooked).

200g short grain sushi rice *rinsed thoroughly in cold water*
2 tablespoons rice wine vinegar
½ tablespoon caster sugar
1 teaspoon sea salt
black sesame seeds
nori (seaweed) squares, to serve (optional)

for the filling
100g very fresh tuna fillet *cut into 5mm dice*
1 tablespoon pickled ginger *finely chopped*
2 spring onions *finely chopped*
1 tablespoon nori (seaweed) flakes
½ teaspoon wasabi paste

inside-out sushi

In one of my mad moments, I decided to reverse the way that sushi is prepared, hence 'inside-out sushi'. I hope you agree that the result looks rather dainty.

1 Place the rice in a pan with 450ml water and bring to the boil. Reduce the heat and cook for 15 minutes, or until just tender. Remove from the heat, cover with a lid, and leave to stand for a further 15 minutes.

2 Transfer the rice to a bowl and add the vinegar, sugar and the salt. Toss together then set aside for the rice to cool.

3 In another bowl, mix together the diced tuna, ginger, spring onions and nori flakes. Add the wasabi and lightly bind the whole lot together.

4 Using wet hands, roll tablespoons of cold rice lightly in the sesame seeds to form small balls. Make a deep indentation in each ball with your finger and push a teaspoon of the tuna mixture into the centre of the rice. Re-form the ball around it.

5 Arrange the stuffed rice balls on squares of nori seaweed (if using), or simply in a deep bowl, and serve at room temperature.

1 ripe avocado (preferably Hass variety)
1 teaspoon pickled ginger *finely chopped*
½ teaspoon wasabi paste
2 spring onions *finely chopped*
juice of 2 limes
2 tablespoons crème fraîche
2 small lotus root
vegetable oil, for deep-frying

asian guacamole

Everyone loves guacamole, the classic Mexican relish. My variation comes from farther afield, with the addition of flavours of the Orient. The lotus root (available in good Asian food shops) makes a great accompaniment, but wonton crisps (see page 170) would work well, too.

1 Cut the avocado in half and remove the stone. Scoop out the flesh into a bowl and mash coarsely with a fork.
2 In another bowl, combine the remaining ingredients and stir gently into the mashed avocado.
3 If not eating the guacamole straight away, you can refrigerate it for up to an hour. If doing so, place the reserved avocado stone in the guacamole (which will stop it turning black), cover with clingfilm and refrigerate.
4 Peel the lotus root and and then slice into 3mm-thick slices using a sharp knife or mandolin. Heat the oil to 160°C/325°F and deep-fry the root for about 1 minute, until golden and crispy. Drain on kitchen paper and cool before serving with the guacamole.

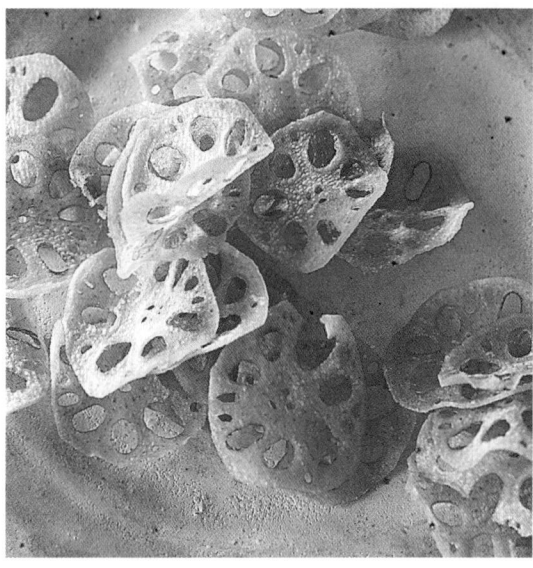

½ **avocado** *peeled and stoned*

⅛ **teaspoon wasabi paste**

2 **tablespoons good-quality mayonnaise**

2cm **piece root ginger** *peeled and grated*

1 **tablespoon yuzu juice (or lime juice)**

1 **tablespoon tomato ketchup**

150g **fresh white crabmeat**

sea salt and freshly ground black pepper

trimmed mustard cress leaves and

salmon caviar, to serve

yuzu crab cocktail

Yuzu is a popular Japanese citrus fruit, a cross between a lime and a tangerine. It has a superb flavour and tastes wonderful in dressings, salsas and sauces. Good oriental stores should sell it, otherwise use lime.

1 Place the avocado and wasabi in a small bowl, and mash to a paste. Place to one side.

2 Combine the mayonnaise, ginger, yuzu (or lime) juice and ketchup to form a sauce. Add the crabmeat and season to taste.

3 To serve, place a spoonful of the mashed avocado in the base of four small cocktail-style martini glasses. Top each with the crab mixture, and garnish with the cress leaves and salmon caviar.

pg tip Wonton crisps make a nice and simple accompaniment to the yuzu crab cocktail. Simply cut the wonton skins in half diagonally, then fry in hot oil at 180°C/350°F, until golden and crispy. Drain on kitchen paper.

asian pesto-grilled chicken

600g chicken breast fillets *boned and skinned*
sea salt and freshly ground black pepper
2 tablespoons chopped mint leaves
3 tablespoons chopped coriander leaves
2 garlic cloves *crushed*
40g roasted peanuts
3cm piece root ginger *peeled and grated*
pinch of sugar
4 tablespoons vegetable oil
extra vegetable oil, for frying
spring onions *thinly sliced, to serve*

This is a simple dish to prepare and delicious to eat. It's also a good way to use up the underfillet of the chicken breast.

1 Cut the chicken fillets into thick strips, then thread them lengthways (satay-style) onto presoaked wooden or bamboo skewers. Place in a shallow dish and season with salt and pepper.
2 Combine the remaining ingredients in a blender and blitz to a coarse pulp. Pour half over the chicken, cover with clingfilm, and marinate for 2–3 hours in the fridge.
3 Brush a grill pan liberally with oil, then place over a high heat. When very hot, place the skewers in the pan and cook gently, turning them regularly, for 4–5 minutes.
4 Arrange the skewers on a dish, pour over the remaining pesto and scatter on the spring onions.

spiced salt and pepper tofu

300g block firm tofu *cut into 2cm cubes*
1 teaspoon black peppercorns
2 teaspoons sea salt
¼ teaspoon Chinese five-spice powder
1 tablespoon plain flour (or cornflour)
vegetable oil *for cooking*

for the peanut sauce
40g roasted peanuts *chopped*
1 tablespoon smooth peanut butter
1 teaspoon *nam pla* (Thai fish sauce)
100ml sweet chilli sauce

If you love tofu, you'll love this recipe. Peanut sauce is my favourite accompaniment, but I occasionally like to serve this with an orange honey sauce (simply warmed honey with some fresh orange juice and zest added), or a spiced soy sauce.

1 To make the peanut sauce, put all the sauce ingredients in a pan, together with 2 tablespoons of water, and heat gently until amalgamated.
2 Place the cubes of tofu between two layers of kitchen paper for about 30 minutes, to remove any excess water.
3 Meanwhile, heat a frying pan and dry fry the peppercorns for about 1 minute, until fragrant. Transfer to a mortar, add the salt and five spice, and crush to a fine powder.
4 Mix the spice mix with the flour in a bowl and use this to coat the tofu cubes, shaking off any excess.
5 Heat a little oil in a wok. When hot, add the tofu cubes in batches and stir-fry until lightly golden. Drain on kitchen paper, then serve with the peanut sauce in a bowl alongside.

200g **raw peeled prawns** *finely chopped or minced*

1 **tablespoon chopped chives**

2 **spring onions** *very finely chopped*

1 **carrot** *peeled and finely chopped or grated*

15g **cornflour**

1 **teaspoon sea salt**

1 **teaspoon sesame oil**

a **pinch of sugar**

6 **medium-size fresh scallops**

12 *gow gee* **wrappers (wonton skins)**

scallop shumai

For a change, feel free to replace the scallop filling for these Chinese dumplings with something else, such as a mixture of minced pork and prawn or chicken. Always serve them with a dipping sauce, even just soy sauce.

1 Place the prawns, chives, spring onions and carrot in a bowl, along with the cornflour. Add the salt, sesame oil and sugar and mix well. Cut the scallops into 1cm dice and add to the bowl.

2 Leave to marinate, covered with clingfilm, for 1 hour.

3 To make the dumplings, first cut the wrappers with a 6–8cm round cutter. Then, lay a circle in the palm of your hand and place a good spoonful of the prawn and scallop mixture in the centre. Bring up the sides of the wrapper to form a nice shape, keeping the top exposed. Prepare all twelve dumplings in the same way.

4 Steam the dumplings in a bamboo-style steamer, over a wok or pan of boiling water, for just 4–5 minutes, or until cooked. Alternatively, cook them gently in a pan of just simmering water.

120g **plain flour**

1 **egg** *beaten*

125ml **beer (lager or any light beer)**

12 **large raw king prawns** *shelled and deveined, tails intact*

75g **unsweetened desiccated coconut**

vegetable oil, for deep-frying

for dipping sauce

3 **tablespoons Chinese mustard (or Dijon mustard)**

1 **teaspoon lemon juice**

2 **tablespoons runny honey**

1 **tablespoon sweet chilli sauce**

beer-battered coconut prawns

Thai coconut prawns are delicious, simple to prepare and quick to be eaten! The beer gives a lightness to the batter, while also adding a yeasty flavour.

1 Make a beer batter from the flour, egg and beer, ensuring that it is nice and smooth.

2 For the sauce, mix all the ingredients together in a pan, then warm through until blended and smooth.

3 Heat the vegetable oil to 160°C/325°F.

4 Dip the prawns in the prepared batter, roll in the coconut, then deep-fry until golden. Drain on kitchen paper then serve with the warm dipping sauce.

butternut cashew pohpiahs

2 tablespoons sesame oil

250g butternut squash *peeled and cut into 1cm cubes*

1 onion *finely chopped*

2.5cm piece root ginger *peeled and finely grated*

2 tablespoons freshly chopped coriander

1 red chilli *deseeded and finely chopped*

4 tablespoons roasted cashew nuts *chopped*

2 tablespoons hoisin sauce (plus extra for serving)

sea salt and freshly ground black pepper

12 spring roll wrappers

1 egg *beaten*

vegetable oil, for deep-frying

Traditionally, these spring rolls are made in Malaysia using a special *pohpiah* dough, a white sticky dough that is skilfully spread over a wok to give an almost translucent skin. You'll be pleased to hear that, for practicality's sake, in my recipe I have used a spring roll pastry, which is just as good.

1 Heat the sesame oil in a wok or frying pan, add the squash cubes and onion, and cook until they begin to soften.

2 Remove from the heat, add the ginger, coriander, chilli and cashews, and stir-fry for 1 minute. Add the hoisin sauce, bind together, and season to taste.

3 Lay out one spring roll wrapper on the work surface, then place a good spoonful of the filling in the centre, leaving a good gap on each side. Brush the two long sides with egg and fold these over to meet in the centre. Then roll the filled pastry tightly away from you, using more egg to hold the closing join together. Prepare all the rolls in the same manner.

4 Heat the oil to 180°C/350°F, then deep-fry the spring rolls until golden and crispy. Drain well on kitchen paper.

5 Serve with hoisin sauce for dipping.

eastern smoked chicken nuggets

2 cooked smoked chicken breasts, skin on

2 tablespoons *kecap manis* (Indonesian soy sauce)

2 garlic cloves *crushed*

2cm piece root ginger *peeled and grated*

2 tablespoons cornflour

½ teaspoon *sansho* pepper (or black pepper, cracked in a mortar)

sea salt

vegetable oil, for deep-frying

lemon wedges, to serve

Sansho pepper, used in the coating of these chicken nuggets, is the Japanese name for Sichuan pepper. It is one of the very few spices used in Japanese cooking and has a pungent, woody aroma and a peppery, slightly citrussy flavour. *Kecap manis* is a favourite Asian ingredient of mine. It has a hint of liquorice which is brilliant in this dish.

1 Cut the chicken breasts into 2–2.5cm cubes and place in a shallow dish. Pour over the Indonesian soy sauce, then add the garlic and ginger and rub liberally all over the chicken pieces. Cover with clingfilm and refrigerate for 30 minutes.

2 Mix the cornflour with the pepper and a little sea salt. Remove the chicken from the marinade and dip in the cornflour.

3 Heat the vegetable oil to 180°C/350°F. When hot, immerse the chicken pieces and fry quickly until golden and crispy.

4 Drain the chicken nuggets on kitchen paper, sprinkle with a little sea salt and serve with lemon wedges.

2 tablespoons vegetable oil (plus extra for deep-frying)

2 spring onions finely chopped

½ teaspoon ground coriander

150g cooked new potatoes *peeled*

50g unsweetened desiccated coconut

8 large king prawns *peeled and deveined, tail intact*

1 tablespoon fresh lime juice

2 teaspoons sesame seeds

8 x 15cm round rice paper wrappers (plus extra in case of tearing)

1 egg white

stuffed prawns in rice skins

Rice papers are very thin, edible paper sheets made from parts of the rice plant. Be patient cooking this recipe as the preparation is definitely fiddly, but worth the effort. Sweet chilli sauce with a dash of soy sauce added makes a good dipping sauce for the prawns.

1 Heat the oil in a wok or frying pan, add the onions and coriander, and cook for 30 seconds. Add the cooked potatoes, breaking them up into a rough mash, and fry together for 3–4 minutes.

2 Stir in the coconut, then remove the potato mixture to a bowl and leave to cool.

3 Toss the prawns with the lime juice and sesame seeds, and leave to marinate for 30 minutes.

4 When the prawns are ready, use a small knife to cut along the back of each one, without cutting right through, to form a butterfly shape. Fill each prawn with some filling, pressing the sides back carefully to close. Push a presoaked satay-size skewer through the bottom of each prawn and out through the top: this will ensure that the prawns keep their shape as they cook.

5 Immerse the rice paper wrappers in water, to soften them, and then dry with a cloth. Brush each wrapper liberally with egg white and use to wrap the prawns. Secure with a cocktail stick.

6 Deep-fry the prawns in oil heated to 180°C/350°F, for 1–2 minutes, until golden and crispy. Drain on kitchen paper before serving.

8 eggs
4 tablespoons vegetable oil
75g shiitake mushrooms *thinly sliced*
1 red chilli *finely chopped*
100g fresh white crabmeat
2 tablespoons roughly chopped
coriander leaves
1 tablespoon soy sauce
to serve: 2 spring onions and 1 banana
shallot, both thinly sliced, and some
fresh coriander leaves

egg fu yung

This dish originated in the city of Shanghai, and was prepared with egg and minced ham. Since the arrival of Chinese chefs in America, many variations have been created using vegetables and seafood.

1 Beat the eggs in a bowl until foamy.

2 Heat a wok or small non-stick frying pan. Add 2 tablespoons of the oil, then throw in the mushrooms and chilli and stir-fry for 1 minute. Add the crabmeat and coriander and heat through. Pour over the soy sauce and mix well together.

3 Pour the remaining oil around the side of the wok then pour over the eggs. Cook over a medium heat, until the egg is lightly golden on the base, then flip the 'omelette' over to cook the top. If you don't fancy flipping the omelette over, you can brown the top under a hot grill.

4 Turn the fu yung onto a plate, sprinkle the sliced spring onions and shallots on top, then scatter over the whole coriander leaves.

200g plain flour
65g self-raising flour
4 tablespoons vegetable oil
4 spring onions, green part only *finely chopped*
2 tablespoons sour cream
125g smoked salmon slices
½ teaspoon wasabi paste
freshly ground black pepper

spring onion pancakes with smoked salmon and wasabi

This recipe takes a common Chinese appetiser and makes it more lavish with the addition of smoked salmon, sour cream and wasabi (hot Japanese horseradish).

1 Bring 200ml water to the boil. Sift the flours in a bowl, then gradually add them to the boiling water, mixing thoroughly all the time.

2 Add sufficient cold water to make a soft pliable dough, then knead this for 2–3 minutes. Return the dough to the bowl, cover with clingfilm, and leave for 30 minutes at room temperature.

3 Divide the dough into two and roll out each half into two large circles, about 3mm thick. Brush the surface with some of the vegetable oil, then sprinkle over the spring onions. Roll up each dough circle into a sausage shape, then cut each sausage into four sections. Re-roll each section into thick round pancakes.

4 Heat some more oil in a non-stick frying pan and fry each pancake for 1–2 minutes on each side, until golden.

5 Spread each pancake liberally with sour cream. Top this with smoked salmon, a dab of wasabi paste and a twist of black pepper, then roll the pancake up.

6 Cut the pancake rolls into pieces before serving.

2 tablespoons groundnut oil

2 garlic cloves *crushed*

4 spring onions *finely chopped*

1 small red chilli *deseeded and finely chopped*

2.5cm piece root ginger *peeled and grated*

1 small red pepper *deseeded and diced*

1 small green pepper *deseeded and diced*

2 tablespoons sake

1 tablespoon light soy sauce

2 tablespoons sweet chilli sauce

1kg fresh mussels *scrubbed and debearded*

wok-roasted mussels

What I adore about mussels, apart from the taste, is the fact that they take no time to cook – a great dish in minutes. Using the wok for this recipe is ideal given the short cooking time.

1 Heat a wok or large frying pan, then add the oil, garlic, spring onions, chilli and ginger, and stir-fry for 10 seconds.

2 Add the peppers, stir-fry for a further 2 minutes, then pour in the sake, soy sauce and chilli sauce. Boil rapidly.

3 Throw in the mussels, cover with a lid and cook for 2–3 minutes, or until the mussels have opened. (Discard any mussels that do not open.) Transfer to a deep serving bowl and serve immediately.

4 red snapper fillets *cleaned and scales removed (mackerel is good, too)*

2 teaspoons sea salt

3cm piece root ginger *peeled and grated*

zest and juice of 1 lemon

4 tablespoons sake

2 tablespoons virgin olive oil

steamed rice, to serve (optional)

sea salt fish with sake and lemon

Japanese salt-grilled fish is one big treat for the taste buds. In Japan, the term *shioyaki* is used to describe the traditional method of salt-grilling beef, poultry or, of course, fish. For me, the best cooking method of any salt-grilled food is quickly over hot coals.

1 Dry the fish fillets on kitchen paper, then make three diagonal slashes into the flesh of each one. Place in a shallow dish.

2 Mix together the salt, ginger and zest and juice of the lemon in a bowl. Pour the mixture over the fish, then leave this to marinate, covered, in the fridge for 30 minutes.

3 Remove the fish from the fridge and sprinkle over the sake, rubbing it liberally but carefully into the flesh.

4 Heat a grill pan until very hot. Brush the fish with olive oil then place on the grill. Cook for 4–5 minutes, turning the fillets over once during cooking. (The cooking time is, of course, dependent on the thickness of the fillets.)

5 Remove from the heat and serve immediately.

beggars' purses

10g dried wild mushrooms
175g ground pork belly
125g freshly picked crabmeat
1 egg *beaten*
3 tablespoons freshly chopped coriander
2.5cm piece root ginger *peeled and finely grated*
2 spring onions *finely chopped*
1 garlic clove *crushed*
sea salt
3 sheets spring roll pastry
a handful of chives (minimum 12)
vegetable oil, for deep-frying

These simple little Chinese pastry purses are filled with pork and crabmeat. If spring roll pastry is not available, wonton skins or even filo pastry would work okay.

1 Just cover the dried mushrooms in boiling water in a bowl, and soak for 20 minutes. Drain and dry them thoroughly, then chop finely.
2 In a bowl, mix together the mushrooms, pork, crab and beaten egg. Stir in the remaining ingredients (except the pastry, chives and oil) and combine well.
3 Cut each of the spring roll sheets into four squares. Put the chives in hot water for 5 seconds to soften, as you'll need these for tying the 'purses'.
4 Place a little of the prepared filling in the centre of each pastry square. Bring up the edges to form a topknot and tie tightly with the softened chives.
5 Heat the vegetable oil to 160°C/325°F, then cook the purses until crisp, golden brown and cooked through. Remove with a slotted spoon and drain on kitchen paper.

pg tip These crispy purses are fantastic served with the following dipping sauce: stir 1 tablespoon sugar into 4 tablespoons warm water. Add 3 tablespoons fish sauce, and 2 tablespoons each of rice wine vinegar and lime juice. Finally, add a clove of crushed garlic and a thinly sliced hot Thai chilli. Allow to infuse for 2 hours before using for the best results.

wok-fried bbq pork

1 egg white
1 tablespoon cornflour
2 tablespoons Shaoxing wine (or dry sherry)
475g pork belly strips *cut into 2.5cm pieces*
3 tablespoons peanut oil
1 garlic clove *crushed*
2.5cm piece root ginger *peeled and grated*
2 spring onions *thinly sliced*
2 red chillies *thinly sliced*
100ml *char siu* (Chinese BBQ sauce)
150ml chicken stock
1 teaspoon soy sauce

Pork belly strips are great in stir-fries as opposed to fillet, which tends to be dry. The natural fat in the belly keeps the meat deliciously juicy.

1 In a bowl, mix together the egg white, cornflour and wine. Add the pork pieces and mix well together.
2 Heat a wok or large frying pan with half the peanut oil. Throw in the pork and stir-fry for 3–4 minutes, until the meat is golden all over. Transfer to a dish.
3 Add the garlic, ginger, spring onions, chillies and remaining peanut oil to the wok and stir-fry for 1 minute. Add the barbecue sauce, stock and soy sauce and cook for a further minute.
4 Return the pork to the sauce, toss to coat and reheat.

Weight (solids)

7g	¼oz
10g	½oz
20g	¾oz
25g	1oz
40g	1½oz
50g	2oz
60g	2½oz
75g	3oz
100g	3½oz
110g	4oz (¼lb)
125g	4½oz
150g	5½oz
175g	6oz
200g	7oz
225g	8oz (½lb)
250g	9oz
275g	10oz
300g	10½oz
310g	11oz
325g	11½oz
350g	12oz (¾lb)
375g	13oz
400g	14oz
425g	15oz
450g	1lb
500g (½kg)	18oz
600g	1¼lb
700g	1½lb
750g	1lb 10oz
900g	2lb
1kg	2¼lb
1.1kg	2½lb
1.2kg	2lb 12oz
1.3kg	3lb
1.5kg	3lb 5oz
1.6kg	3½lb
1.8kg	4lb
2kg	4lb 8oz
2.25kg	5lb
2.5kg	5lb 8oz
3kg	6lb 8oz

Volume (liquids)

5ml	1 teaspoon
10ml	1 dessertspoon
15ml	1 tablespoon or ½fl oz
30ml	1fl oz
40ml	1½fl oz
50ml	2fl oz
60ml	2½fl oz
75ml	3fl oz
100ml	3½fl oz
125ml	4fl oz
150ml	5fl oz (¼ pint)
160ml	5½fl oz
175ml	6fl oz
200ml	7fl oz
225ml	8fl oz
250ml (0.25 litre)	9fl oz
300ml	10fl oz (½ pint)
325ml	11fl oz
350ml	12fl oz
370ml	13fl oz
400ml	14fl oz
425ml	15fl oz (¾ pint)
450ml	16fl oz
500ml (0.5 litre)	18fl oz
550ml	19fl oz
600ml	20fl oz (1 pint)
700ml	1¼ pints
850ml	1½ pints
1 litre	1¾ pints
1.2 litres	2 pints
1.5 litres	2½ pints
1.8 litres	3 pints
2 litres	3½ pints

Length

5mm	¼in
1cm	½in
2cm	¾in
2.5cm	1in
3cm	1¼in
4cm	1½in
5cm	2in
7.5cm	3in
10cm	4in
15cm	6in
18cm	7in
20cm	8in
24cm	10in
28cm	11in
30cm	12in

Oven temperatures

Celsius*/Fahrenheit   Gas/Description

110°C/225°F	mark ¼/cool
130°C/250°F	mark ½/cool
140°C/275°F	mark 1/very low
150°C/300°F	mark 2/very low
170°C/325°F	mark 3/low
180°C/350°F	mark 4/moderate
190°C/375°F	mark 5/mod. hot
200°C/400°F	mark 6/hot
220°C/425°F	mark 7/hot
230°C/450°F	mark 8/very hot

*For fan-assisted ovens, reduce temperatures by 10°

acknowledgements Firstly I would like to thank my family for their understanding whilst I've been engrossed at weekends writing this book. *Thanks also go to:* Lara Mand who works wonders, deciphering my scrawls on paper and somehow translating them into order! Linda Tubby, good friend and home economist who knows me so well, and translates my ideas and recipes perfectly onto the plate. Pete Cassidy, for once again, some wonderful photography. Róisín Nield and Helen Trent for capturing the mood with their superb props. Jane Humphrey for laying out the pages so beautifully. Jane Middleton for her continued support and friendship on the project. Barry Tomkinson, one of my many young and talented chefs of the future, for his help with recipe testing and preparation. Friends Glenn Ewart of Churchill China Plc and Paul Goodfellow of Continental Chef Supplies for help with certain glassware and chinaware for the photography. A special thank you to Jennifer Wheatley, project editor and Emily Hatchwell, copy editor, for your enthusiasm and encouragement with my ideas. You both have been a real pleasure to work with.

photographic acknowledgements All photography by Peter Cassidy except for the following: page 4 and 70 Neil Emmerson / Getty Images; 10 Brand X Pictures / Alamy; 40 Andrea Pistolesi / Getty Images; 100 Stuart Westmorland / Getty Images; 130 Beth Callahan / Alamy; 154 Jeff Spielman / Getty Images